ADVANCE PRAISE FOR
POWER UP

"This book is a must-read for anyone in business. *Power UP* gives real, actionable advice on how to charter your own destiny, especially when the odds are stacked against you."

—JULIE WAINWRIGHT, founder and CEO of The RealReal

"Magdalena and I worked together in the early days of the Internet, introducing concepts that were completely revolutionary, such as the electronic wallet. She is a fearless entrepreneur who worked hard to help early online merchants get off the ground. Some of them went on to become giants, like Amazon. I urge women to be bold like Magdalena and follow their dreams."

—ERIC SCHMIDT, executive chairman of Google and parent company Alphabet

"I wish I could have given Magdalena Yeşil's book to my two daughters when they graduated from college. It's the perfect gift for any young woman navigating her career. I am definitely giving it to my two girls, and just as importantly, to their boyfriends, too.

—STEVE BLANK, entrepreneur and author of *The Startup Owner's Manual* and *Four Steps to Epiphany*

"My professional mission is to empower women through fashion. *Power UP* resonated strongly with me. I highly recommend its confident career guidance from an impressive roster of top women leaders."

—KAREN WATKINS, COO of Christian Dior

"When I reached out to Magdalena in my early days of founding Pono, I benefited greatly from her wisdom and guidance. She is a pragmatic, down-to-earth person who helped me a lot."

—NEIL YOUNG, composer, musician, and founder of digital music startup Pono

"*Power UP* offers the no-nonsense optimism and encouragement women need to persevere in technology, an industry where so much is stacked against them. It's crammed with sage advice and insider stories to enlighten the next generation of women in tech."

—ADRIANA GASCOIGNE, founder and CEO of Girls in Tech

"This book should be required reading for anyone building a company or making a career as we head into the Fourth Industrial Revolution. The lessons Magdalena Yeşil offers from her remarkable work pioneering the commercial Internet are more relevant than ever."

—MURAT SÜNMEZ, member of the
World Economic Forum Managing Board

"Technology is changing how business is conducted in all industries. Women who seize technology-related opportunities and put the advice offered in *Power UP* to work will confidently transform businesses and emerge as future leaders of the new economy."

—RON CONWAY, founder of SVAngel

"Magdalena Yeşil offers powerful leadership lessons from her journey to becoming a successful Silicon Valley entrepreneur and investor. She drops the reader into vividly recounted, career-defining moments to help them navigate and overcome gender bias in their own lives."

—CAROLINE SIMARD, senior director of research at the
Clayman Institute for Gender Research at Stanford University

POWER UP

POWER UP

How Smart Women Win
in the New Economy

MAGDALENA YEŞIL

with SARA GRACE

SEAL PRESS

Da Capo Press
Hachette Book Group
1290 Avenue of the Americas, New York, NY 10104
www.dacapopress.com
@DaCapoPress, @DaCapoPR

Printed in the United States of America
First Edition: October 2017

Published by Da Capo Press, an imprint of Perseus Books, LLC,
a subsidiary of Hachette Book Group, Inc.

The Hachette Speakers Bureau provides a wide range of authors for speaking events.
To find out more, go to www.hachettespeakersbureau.com or call (866) 376-6591.
The publisher is not responsible for websites (or their content)
that are not owned by the publisher.

Editorial production by Lori Hobkirk at the Book Factory.
Print book interior design by Cynthia Young at Sagecraft.

Library of Congress Cataloging-in-Publication Data has been applied for.
ISBNs: 978-1-58005-691-5 (hardcover), 978-1-58005-692-2 (ebook)

LSC-C

10 9 8 7 6 5 4 3 2 1

To Kevork Yeşil,
the man who believed in me more than anyone
else ever has or will. Thank you, Dad, for giving me
the gift of self-confidence and for teaching me to stand on
my own two legs, no matter how wobbly.
I will forever cherish our eighteen years together.

CONTENTS

FOREWORD

By Marc Benioff

When Magdalena Yeşil first asked me to write the foreword for *Power UP*, my reaction was, "Are you sure? Wouldn't another woman who has broken the glass ceiling be the more appropriate choice for a book written for women on how to succeed and lead in today's business world?"

"No," Magdalena told me in her indomitable way. "It should be you. After all, gender is not a just a woman's issue." Which is, of course, true. How could I say no? Magdalena's story traces back to the earliest days of Salesforce and her role in helping us launch the company, survive the dot-com bust, and enter the public market with our IPO.

Magdalena and I first met in 1994. She quickly became a friend, adviser, and then the first investor in Salesforce. She immediately understood our vision to revolutionize the software industry with a new technology model, delivering business software via the cloud; a new business model, buying software on a subscription basis; and a new integrated philanthropic model, donating 1 percent of Salesforce's product, 1 percent of Salesforce's equity, and 1 percent of employees' time to help nonprofits achieve their missions.

And with her clear-eyed focus and direct style, she let me know when she felt it was time to go bigger, to bring in other investors, and even for me to finally cut the cord with Oracle, where I had worked for thirteen years. I've told these stories in my own book

Behind the Cloud, and here you get Magdalena's side of the story. I can tell you that at pivotal times in my own career I followed Magdalena's advice and appreciated her fearless, practical approach to all that came our way. We started out as ten people crammed into a small San Francisco apartment in 1999, and now Salesforce is a Fortune 500 company with more than twenty-five thousand people driving customer success for 150,000-plus companies around the world.

Although her professional stories and successes are many, it's her personal story here that inspires me. As a hardworking immigrant who came to America from Turkey in the late 1970s, Magdalena has a uniquely American success story. Through perseverance, determination, and an unwavering belief in her own talent, Magdalena forged a path, first in the technology industry and then venture capital at a time when not many women did.

A more diverse and inclusive workplace is critical to building the most innovative products and successful companies. The tech industry in particular has been under fire for its lack of diversity, particularly when it comes to women and underrepresented minorities in leadership and technology roles. The World Economic Forum estimates that it will take up to 170 years for the world's women to earn wages equitable to men's.

In *Power UP* Magdalena now shares her journey as well as those of other female leaders who have made it to the top, providing a guide for other women navigating their careers at any level and within any industry. With her fearless attitude and experience as a woman thriving in Silicon Valley's super-competitive environment, Magdalena offers her take on dealing with gender bias, knowing your value, taking risks, and bouncing back from failure. She makes the case for men and women working together to design the workplace of the future, looking out for one another with a sense of compassion and gratitude.

With equal parts practical advice and inspiration, *Power UP* both challenges and empowers readers to take control of their own careers. As I can attest, you'll have an advantage with Magdalena beside you on your journey.

Introduction

THERE'S A WOMAN
IN THE MEN'S ROOM

In the fall of 2015 I chaired the Innovation Summit at the G20 conference in Antalya, Turkey, where presidents, prime ministers, finance and labor ministers, and leading research and policy institutions from the top twenty economies in the world had gathered to discuss global financial problems. This was the first time the G20 had put innovation and technology on the agenda, so there was a lot of attention focused on the Innovation Summit.

In addition to chairing the summit I was also asked to participate on a panel exploring how to help small and medium enterprises (SMEs) experience faster growth in a slowing global new economy.

After the panel discussion was over, the moderator invited questions from the audience. The first question was directed at me, and it did not have anything to do with SME; instead, someone asked whether I had faced difficulties and challenges in Silicon Valley because I was a woman.

I wasn't surprised. This wasn't the first time in my thirty-year career I had been on stage to discuss a business issue and immediately gotten a question about my gender.

I responded with a somewhat contrarian take, saying that I couldn't think of a single door that was permanently shut to me because I was a woman—and that in fact being a woman in the predominantly male technology world had opened many doors to me. Although that's entirely true, it's also true that being a woman created many painful challenges for me to navigate, often alone. But that was never where I focused my attention, and a forum on increasing growth in the global economy didn't seem the moment to start.

Another woman on the panel, a leading researcher from a German think tank, chimed in next. She had just completed a multiyear study of small and medium enterprises around the world and recited a litany of depressing statistics about the very real barriers holding women back: limited access to initial and growth capital, limited representation in the corporate executive suite, limited networking capability because of exclusion from gendered social activities, and on and on.

After the panel the German researcher immediately approached me. "You know what?" she said. "Listening to you, I couldn't help but think that the reason you were successful as a woman in a men's world was because you didn't focus at all on the statistics and facts I was quoting. In fact, you ignored them completely. You proceeded in your career as though you had as much chance at success as anybody else—or maybe even more."

She was right, and what she said perfectly summarized what I now see as the key to my path to power as a woman in Silicon Valley. If I had stopped to think about being in the minority—with the numbers against me, at risk of discrimination—I might have lost the courage to go out and compete with the best. Like a motorcyclist, I've never ignored the rocks and debris that could send me skidding, but I've never focused on them either. I set my sights then and now on the smooth ground that allows me to move ahead. Otherwise the fear of crashing might overwhelm me. My background was no doubt a major influence. Growing up as a Christian kid in a 99 percent Muslim country had taught me to focus not on my differences but rather on my strengths.

That day at the Summit I realized something important that sometimes gets lost in the conversation about gender: gender still matters, but we can't let it matter too much. In doing so, we risk shifting too much of our focus—and others'—from our achievements to our gender. I believe that's part of why many successful, pioneering women in Silicon Valley whom I asked to be a part of this book declined. Some gave elaborate reasons, others kept it brief, but I often heard the same message in their responses: "I got where I am because I did not focus on being a woman but rather on being the best I could. I won because of my talent, hard work, and determination. I never let my gender define me, and I don't want to start doing that now."

I immediately understood their response, as I have always taken that same stance. I always acted as though—and in fact believed—my gender did not matter and I belonged in every room, no matter what anybody else might think. And yet the fact that three decades after I started my own career the conditions for women pursuing careers in technology have hardly changed tells me it's time that we who have been successful step up and explicitly, publicly support the next generation making their way in this tough field. That means owning that being a woman in the new economy is different from being a man in the new economy, with its own set of challenges to overcome.

That said, when I say I thought I belonged in *every* room, I mean it. Once I was the only woman serving on a company's board of directors that had convened to discuss a particularly heated issue, one of those "bet the company"–level decisions. The conversation was fast and furious and lasted a good part of the day. At one point one of the gentlemen called for a break.

We walked down the hallway together while I wrapped up a passionate point. Then the men opened a door, and we all walked through it.

The door shut behind us, and suddenly all eyes were wide on me. For a split second I wondered if what I was saying was completely off the wall or somehow too complicated for them to follow. Then I took in our surroundings: Florescent lighting. Tiled floors. Urinals. Men using urinals.

I had walked into the men's bathroom.

Without stopping to comment on our whereabouts, I finished my sentence, gave a casual nod, and walked out. On my way to the women's bathroom I considered whether to be embarrassed. But mostly I felt annoyed because I was sure they were continuing the conversation without me, and I didn't want to miss out or have to catch up.

When we reconvened in the boardroom, the mood was more relaxed. *Great*, I thought, *they already came to a decision.*

"So did you guys finish the discussion?" I asked.

They all smiled.

"Magdalena, we didn't talk about the company at all," one of them said. "All we could talk about was that you had walked into the bathroom! We were shocked, but not you—you didn't even *react*. All you cared about was finishing your point! You're completely unflappable."

His tone was admiring, and we all laughed. Then we got back to the business at hand, which was actually much more productive now that everyone's mood had lightened.

With this book I want to help the next generation of women look blithely past the poor odds to power UP and command the right to be in any room. I want to help you look beyond the gender statistics of the workplace and feel confident entering any of the technology-related fields—but also prepared to deal with the challenges.

Although I urge women to focus on the smooth road to ride fast and fearless, I will also talk about some of the tough circumstances we do face. It's not talked about enough, particularly among women who have made it. I want women to have tools to manage the people who, consciously or unconsciously, act to take away their power. I'm sharing these stories for men as well because I believe the next big push forward shouldn't be a women's movement—it'll take all of us.

This is not a research book or a political platform but a field guide for women who want to have successful careers in the new economy at large. I don't want women to have illusions about the tradeoffs inherent in a hard-driving career. High-growth business means cultures that don't coddle people. They're not particularly attentive to work-life balance. They're high risk.

Those are the downsides. The upsides are work that is intellectually stimulating, relationships that feed off the shared thrill of creating something new, and a shot at wealth and opportunity way beyond what's readily available in most other fields.

THE TIME IS NOW

Technology is the driving force of the New Economy. With the creative use of technology, established industries are being transformed, creating new competitors who are emerging as leaders. Great examples of new-economy companies are AirBnB, ZipCar, and Facebook, three companies that are changing the way people vacation, get from one place to another, and create and consume information. The new economy is coming to an industry and an office near you, opening the floodgates for mainstream participation.

All this suggests a unique opportunity for women to power UP, changing both the face and the future of technology. High-growth startups create lots of jobs and typically make their employees owners. Even the company cook can become a millionaire, as we witnessed when Google went public. These companies are more willing to break rules than are legacy firms because they have little to protect. With good ideas, courage, and hard work, workers in the new economy can leap hierarchies, bypass gatekeepers, and upend traditional expectations around success. And because these companies will be breaking a lot of established norms and redefining processes, they are by nature open to new ideas, both from men and from women.

Furthermore, to succeed in the new economy, you don't need to be an engineer or a person enthralled by technology for technology's sake. Think about a company like Rent the Runway, which is using sophisticated logistics and distribution to make couture fashion accessible to women who can't afford to buy it. Underneath all the sparkling gowns, it's an impressive technology company.

I I I

THE CULTURE OF TECHNOLOGY IS CHANGING. New-economy leaders are now owning the ways that privilege, gender, and race have shut people out of otherwise healthy meritocracies. There's a lot of work to do. You have only to look at my own Valley network, from which the women in this book were drawn, to see this is true. They are brilliant, driven, and deserving of their opportunities. They are also predominantly white or from privileged educational backgrounds. By and large this is still the face of Silicon Valley. But change is coming, with leaders recognizing that diversity leads to better results: stronger, more innovative teams, and better products and services for customers.

At the time I came of age in high tech there were so few women that we weren't thinking about a political movement. We were doing what we needed to get work done in a man's world. We were not thinking about whether we had it hard—and we certainly weren't thinking about whether there might be others who had it even harder. Essentially I ignored my gender and focused on my success. Other women took the same approach. When Kate Mitchell, the cofounder of Scale Ventures and board member of the National Venture Capital Association, recently told an audience of women in San Francisco that she had finally decided "to come out as a woman" after years of doing whatever she could do to minimize her gender differences to fit into the male-dominated technology world, many women nodded their heads.

Today women and men have much higher expectations for how workplaces address bias, recruit talent, and create an environment that makes everybody feel comfortable and confident. We're also seeing the fruit of many decades of politics and formal advocacy. The numbers may still weigh against women, but major companies such as Salesforce and Amazon have publicly set goals and announced they've achieved pay parity, a victory that third-party salary surveys have confirmed. More companies and victories for equal pay and opportunity will surely follow. Academics, politicians, and entrepreneurs are all working to increase the number of women working in high-tech and STEM fields more broadly.

But let's put all that back in our peripheral vision. I was compelled to write this book because I believe that there's another, much more powerful reason that every woman reading is poised to power UP:

> Within each of us lies 100 percent of the capability needed to overcome the obstacles to any goal we set for ourselves. You are much more powerful than you think.

Powering UP, as I see it, requires you to own your power. Powered-UP women:

▌ **BECOME THEIR OWN PRIMARY ENERGY SOURCE.** You can't rely on someone else to boost your confidence, elevate your mood, or set your agenda. Everyone has days when that's easy, but those who succeed are the ones who can find ways to sustain their self-confidence on the days that are incredibly hard. When your confidence comes from within you, you gain the ability to face difficult people and situations without shutting down, losing control, or becoming bitter or resentful.

▌ **REFUSE TO ACCEPT THE RULES AS THEY ARE WRITTEN.** Note that I didn't call this book *Level Up*. Leveling up suggests climbing an existing hierarchy. Its focus is outward, deferring to the rules by which power and influence are currently distributed. Powering UP is about being so strongly grounded in your sense of self and what you have to offer that people rewrite those rules for you—and when they don't, you build spaces in which you have the authority to rewrite them yourself. You create new opportunity rather than scramble to get your piece of what's already there.

▌ **NEVER DEFINE THEMSELVES BY GENDER OR ANY OTHER EXCLUSION PARAMETER OR ALLOW ANYONE ELSE TO DO THE SAME.** The moment you *see* yourself as a victim is the moment you become one. But believe in yourself as a winner and prove it to others around you, and soon others will be competing to have you on their team.

This book has been made possible by the many brave women founders and technology leaders who have joined me in putting out their hands to pull other women up. This is the final level of powering UP: finding ways to help others who have never gotten a fair shake—not just women but everyone who has been either overlooked or judged inadequate by the reigning gatekeepers.

We can all power UP, no matter how low our beginnings or how big our challenges. Powering UP beats all other alternatives. And when enough of us have powered up, we'll just knock down the gates.

The Power to Flow

I've come to believe that powering UP in business isn't about smarts or even about the desire to succeed. Particularly in the high-stakes game of entrepreneurship, power comes from having the courage to fail. It may feel counterintuitive to talk about failure before we've even addressed success, but actually that's the order that mirrors the real world: you often fail ten times so you can succeed once. Although most people think of me as a Silicon Valley success story, I can't tell you how many times I hit a wall over the course of my life and my career, making terrible mistakes and failing miserably, often because I had absolutely no idea what I was doing.

In Turkey, where I'm from, we have a tradition: when someone embarks on a major journey the whole neighborhood shows up to throw buckets of water behind them as they walk or drive away. It's a way of saying, "May you be like water—easily flowing past any obstacle." I have often thought of that ritual as I have moved forward on my life journey. There are no failures, only obstacles. Whatever the obstacles, I find a way to flow. And even as water can be gentle, it can also have great power. Instead of the stream, imagine the thundering, disruptive power of a waterfall.

Take my first big move, from Turkey to the United States, to go to college—a fall into the unknown. Nothing about the application process was easy in those days before the Internet. I was seventeen years old. No one in my family had ever gone to college, and those I knew who did go to college went to the universities in Turkey. Most of the information I had on American education came from a single thick book in my school's library titled *Colleges and Universities of the United States*.

I would have to take the SAT before I could apply, I learned. Istanbul is a city built on two continents, Europe and Asia, and a body of water called the Bosphorus divides them. The SAT exam was being offered on the European side of Istanbul at a very early hour before the ferries started running—a problem for me, as I lived on the Asian side. I figured I'd find a way. First I had to find someone who would accompany me in getting to the exam in the middle of the night, and my father, who was not keen on my going to the United States on my own, had not volunteered. I asked my boyfriend, who obliged, despite having nothing to gain from my leaving the country: I'd be leaving him behind.

Before dawn we made our way to the narrowest part of the Bosphorus and found a fisherman sleeping on his boat. We woke him up, and he motored us across the channel, where he left us to find our way to the SAT testing venue up the hill. Once in the exam room I was amazed to see that the multiple-choice test required you to color in a circle to specify your answer. I had never seen such a test before.

I asked the SAT organization to send my scores to the two schools I had applied to, chosen from the big university book: California Institute of Technology and Massachusetts Institute of Technology (MIT). Shortly after, the SAT organization wrote to me, stating that they would send my scores to a third school free of charge. I went back to the big book and found a third school that rhymed with the first two, Illinois Institute of Technology. Without anything better to guide me, I chose it because I saw it was close to a big lake, and I like water.

As soon as my high SAT scores came in, Illinois Institute of Technology sent me an acceptance letter without even asking me for a complete application. I was so delighted that they liked me so much that I accepted their offer. As far as I knew, it was similar in caliber to MIT, so I was not inclined to wait to hear MIT's reply.

This was career mistake number one.

I arrived at the O'Hare Airport in Chicago a few months later excited and hopeful. I was living a dream that had origins back when I was ten and happened to catch the *Apollo 11* moon landing, broadcast on a US military radio station that I often tuned into because they played American music. I didn't speak much English, but the excited voices of the broadcasters told me everything I needed to know: America was a place—maybe the only place—where not even the sky was the limit. And not only were they sending men to the moon, they were doing it wearing blue jeans! I was still a kid and didn't know exactly what I wanted to do with my life, but I knew the frontier was what exhilarated me and the United States represented the edge. It was the place where the impossible became possible. From that day on, I wanted to go to America. No, from that day on, *I was going to go to America.* And now I had done it!

▪ ▪ ▪

MISTAKE NUMBER ONE might not have been so bad had Illinois Institute been located in a safe part of town. But it was in South Side Chicago, right in the middle of the projects. Coming from Princes' Islands, in the sea of Marmara outside Istanbul, where we rarely locked our doors, that was quite a transition.

I arrived at my new home, a campus dorm room, late in the evening. I was starving after the twenty-seven-hour journey from Istanbul and asked my new dorm mates when dinner would be served. They told me that the cafeteria had long closed. Panicked, I asked if there was anywhere to get food, and they suggested a McDonald's two blocks away.

Famished, I left immediately, not bothering to change from my elegant "going to America" travel clothes—high heels, pleated skirt, and eight gold bracelets to sell if I needed emergency cash. Halfway to the restaurant a police cruiser pulled over alongside me. Was I already in trouble with the police? I had only just arrived! I wondered what I could have done wrong. I kept walking, acting as if I did not notice the police car.

The officer who was driving called out to me from his window.

"Ma'am, where are you going dressed like that?" he asked.

In my fairly heavy British accent I replied, "Sir, I am going to a restaurant named McDonalds."

He stopped the cop car and rolled down his window all the way. "Get in the back," he ordered. "We'll take you—and don't you ever go walking alone around here again. Plus, take off those gold bracelets and put them in a safe place. They could get you stabbed or killed." The cops not only escorted me into McDonald's, but they also helped me order my food, then delivered me back to my dorm.

That night, still in shock, I called my dad in Istanbul and told him what had happened.

"Dad," I said, "you were correct. America is a very scary and dangerous place. The police told me I would be mugged or even killed for just walking down the street to get dinner. I'm going to change the date on my round-trip ticket and come back home right away. Obviously this was a very huge mistake."

Instead of getting sympathy and support from the man who had warned me not to go to America, my dad said what I least expected.

"This was your idea," he said. "You were excited to go. Trust in yourself. Have confidence that you can handle anything. Do not get intimidated so easily. You should stick with the decision you made for at least a year to let it play out. It is way too early to quit on your lifelong ambition."

And after telling me he had no doubt I could learn to live safely in my new environment if I did what the police told me to do, he hung up.

Without knowing it, my father had just told me to power UP.

When I went home for summer break at the end of the school year my father confessed to me that he could not sleep for months, sick with worry about my safety. But he never let me feel that during my yearlong stay in Chicago. All I heard from him while I was at IIT was how much he trusted my judgment and maturity to endure any situation. He wanted me to power UP and make the best of my first year in America.

Meanwhile he had been right to worry. IIT was truly in one of Chicago's worst neighborhoods. Every day we heard a story of someone getting mugged on his or her way to class. I was never one of these victims, possibly because I took the police officers' advice and changed the way I dressed, became aware of my surroundings, and locked my jewelry away. Newly street-smart, I turned my attention to my professors, fellow students, and the exciting business of learning—what I had come all this way to do.

■   ■   ■

AS FALL TURNED into winter, another big mistake became clear. I had arrived in Chicago with two suitcases of clothes perfect for the modest Mediterranean winter in Turkey but completely inappropriate for the subzero climes of Chicago. My work-study job was to deliver mail between the different departments, and as I hustled around the frigid campus I really believed I might die or, at the very least, lose my nose. Even though I was relatively happy with my classes at IIT and had already made the Dean's List, I decided very quickly that Chicago's winter was not for me. Every gust of wind as I walked the campus made it seem even more a matter of survival.

One day I heard two students in the cafeteria talking about how they missed the warm weather in California. I got their attention.

"Are there good schools in California?" I asked.

It turned out they were from Northern California, so they mentioned Stanford and Berkeley. Soon I was knee-deep in the application process to become a transfer student.

Still, it wasn't easy. The night before my applications were due I had my roommate read my application essay. She shook her head at the handwritten pages.

"You can't send this," she said.

"Why not?" I asked.

She stared at me, completely bewildered. "You can't tell them that the reason you want to attend Stanford University is because you want to be where the weather is warm! That's ridiculous! It's one of the best schools in the country."

"But that's the truth!" I said. "What else am I supposed to say?"

She was exasperated with me.

"And half the words are spelled wrong!" she said, pushing the paper back at me.

Later I'd learn that this lifelong struggle with spelling was the result of being severely dyslexic. But in any case, I'd handwritten the application because I did not know how to type. And there was no time to get a new form and start fresh, so I sent my applications to Stanford and Berkeley without making any changes. By some miracle—and my solid academic record—both Stanford and Berkeley accepted me as a transfer student for my sophomore year. I chose Stanford.

I was much happier in California and on a much stronger path to learning what I needed to know about myself and the world around me. Still, I would go on to make many other mistakes. I chose the wrong major. (Pre-med was my father's dream, but the cutthroat environment and rote memorization weren't for me—I switched to engineering.) I declined a job offer to become a very early Apple employee after interviewing with both Steve Wozniak and Steve Jobs and liking both of them a lot. (My master's adviser told me not to take a job from a technology company that had a fruit for its name, so I passed on the Apple offer to work at Advanced Micro Devices.) Later in my career I failed to find investors for my first startup. (It was focused on commercializing the Internet, which at the time was such a revolutionary idea that venture capitalists didn't get it.)

What all these moments had in common was that when I made a mistake or got stuck—a positive if sometimes painful sign that you're entering uncharted territory—I never got discouraged;

instead, I'd power UP and find the crack through which I could flow to a newer and stronger source.

And so, amid many mistakes, I gradually built a track record of successes. I dropped pre-med, where I was struggling, and switched to engineering, where I thrived in a more collaborative atmosphere. That failed startup? It folded into a company called UUNet, where we eventually had a very successful initial public offering. And two decades later, when Steve Jobs went back to Apple for the second time, he came calling again—and again I turned him down, this time with a nuanced understanding of the opportunity I was declining and with the confidence that I was making the right choice for the right reasons (more about that later).

■ ■ ■

I'M SHARING THESE stories because any woman breaking the glass ceiling in the new economy—or, really, any man or woman breaking new ground—needs to be prepared to persist through mistakes and outright failures. Many will be your own doing. Others might befall you because of the barriers people throw in your way. The key to my success was being unafraid and always finding a way to flow forward.

I believe that no field in the world is as welcoming to outliers and underdogs as the technology industry. Technology always looks to the future, allowing you to trade on your potential rather than your past. If you have the potential and the determination, doors will open to you. All you need is the courage to fail—which I believe comes so much more easily once you see that failing is part of every successful person's story.

I always gave myself permission to make big bets and lose several. The more bets you survive—win *or* lose—the more your confidence grows and your ability to power UP increases.

AUDACITY,
OR A DELICIOUS EFF-YOU ATTITUDE

Confidence matters. Recently I listened with regret as a venture capitalist told me that she had watched a woman entrepreneur pitch a fantastic company, hoping to raise $2 million. Next she heard a pitch from the male CEO of a struggling, all-but-failed company—and he had the balls to ask for $10 million!

Sadly I have seen this too often: women often cautiously round down on their ambitions and asks, while men round up. If we want to be given equal opportunity and full credit, we need to stop underestimating ourselves. And if others underestimate us, we need to dial up our audacity.

> Any woman breaking the glass ceiling in the new economy—or, really, any man or woman breaking new ground—needs to be prepared to persist through mistakes and outright failures.

My first engineering job was as a product designer. I clearly remember one of my first design review meetings. I had done good, careful work and felt proud and accomplished when I sat down with my boss and the review team to present the logic functions of the semiconductor chip I was designing.

The review team had its own point of view on my work. For thirty minutes they criticized my design, and not always constructively. Their litany of complaints was harsh and detailed. I listened carefully, ignoring the tone and taking notes.

After the meeting my boss asked me, "So how do you feel?"

"I think it went pretty well," I replied.

"Were we in the same meeting?" he said in disbelief. "They ripped your work apart, and they weren't nice about it either. That couldn't have felt good."

"I'll make the changes now that I understand what they want. But I still see the value in the work I did, and I'm still proud of it— whether they liked it or not!"

My boss shook his head at me, smiling.

"Magdalena, I don't know where you got that delicious eff-you attitude, but I like it. You don't let anything get to you!"

In his eyes this "delicious" attitude became a defining aspect of how I worked, and he referred to it often. As for the "eff you," it wasn't quite accurate. I was unflappable, not defiant—but in the corporate environment of that company the two were close enough for my boss to enjoy the joke, and the label stuck.

My delicious attitude was a huge asset. It allowed me to accept criticism, negative feedback, and any other unflattering input during meetings without becoming defensive or bent out of shape. I was able to process the feedback while keeping my enthusiasm and positivity intact. My colleagues could sense I was comfortable, so they never censored themselves to protect against a bad reaction. This was a big advantage because they wielded the feedback that I needed so I could improve.

My first boss was also noticing something essential about the way I operate to this day: I never doubt my own value. Not everything I do is perfect, nor are all my ideas great, but knowing that—or having someone else point it out to me!—doesn't upset my self-esteem. Also, an idea or solution can be a good one but not the right one for the moment. Accordingly, I don't need to dig my heels in when someone asks me to change, as in the case of my design review. When you believe that your own opinion matters most, you always feel comfortable hearing feedback, even when it's negative. I take what I need to improve, and then I move on. I try to make sure that the ground beneath me is so solid that I'm ready to walk somewhere new when I need to.

I'm also never afraid to put myself out there with an audacious request. Shortly after we had founded CyberCash, when we were still a no-name company, I found myself in a meeting with Stewart Alsop, the organizer of the technology industry's elite invite-only AGENDA conference. At the time it was the most exclusive annual event for the industry, full of people like Bill Gates and Larry Ellison. I was a founder of a tiny company, and there was no way I would be on their invite list. Until that moment the organizer had never heard of me or my company. But as our meeting drew to a close and I shook Stewart's hand goodbye, I said, "You know, my birthday is coming up, and do you know what I really want for my birthday?"

He was startled. But he took the bait and asked me what I wanted.

"I want to be a speaker at your conference."

We both laughed, and I let it pass as a joke. Six months later CyberCash had made great progress. We were working with Eric Schmidt and his team at Sun Microsystems, and we were all over the media as the first secure payment system for the new Internet startups starting to sell products online. Amidst the excitement I got an email from Stewart offering me a seat as a panelist at the AGENDA conference along with Scott Cook, the founder and chairman of Intuit, and two other CEOs from the credit card and banking industries.

"Your comment earlier got me to thinking," he wrote. "We don't have any women panelists, and you're perfect for this financial services panel." In that moment being a woman was a huge advantage, and I was happy to have it work for me.

Then as now, seats are available to women—but you can't wait to be asked. It works a lot better and more often if you get out in front and ask for the seat.

GRATITUDE KEEPS YOU FLOWING

Although audacity is your friend, entitlement is not. The secret to balancing the two is gratitude. This is the gentler aspect of water, the part that gives.

As an immigrant, I found that this balance came naturally to me. I was grateful to be here in America, grateful for an education on a beautiful campus, grateful for a work permit and a job, grateful for every little break I got. No one in this country owed me anything; I had no expectations. If anything, I expected I'd have to work twice as hard as everyone else. Anyone who helped me, whether they were offering advice or opening a door, could see pure happiness and appreciation written across my face—which made them want to help me more. Still, I never took anything for granted; I was entitled to nothing.

Gratitude, I believe, contributed the "delicious" to my "eff-you attitude." To be successful you need both. If I had been antagonistic or unwilling to listen to and truly hear anything negative—a *real* "eff-you attitude"—I would have washed out fast. But I wasn't any of those things. I was the opposite. Because I came to the United States as an international college student, I was in learner mode from day one. Feedback *was* delicious to me. I listened openly and believed it was natural and in no way shameful that I had many things to learn or change about my work.

Immigrants like me, I've come to believe, are predisposed to be *humbitious*, the term coined by researchers at Bell Labs for the blend

Focusing on what others think can waste a lot of time and energy that would be better used moving yourself ahead. Of course what your boss or a significant player in management thinks of you is important, and you need to pay attention. But many of us spend a lot of time worrying about what others think without assessing why their thoughts are relevant. The most important opinion about you is your own. Think highly of yourself and your work, and then convince others why they should agree.

of humility and ambition they found to be common among the most effective scientists and engineers in their organization. Ambition propels you forward, but humility keeps you grounded and your mind open to learning.

My reality is that I never felt resentful that I had to work twice or three times as hard as anyone else to make progress. I was truly grateful for the opportunity to be in America, regardless of how my workload compared to others around me. In fact, I never made the comparison; I focused on my own forward momentum. Bosses, colleagues, my team, and my staff noticed and appreciated my sense of gratitude and rewarded me in return. And as I have matured in my career and achieved more, the reality that I am really blessed to have the opportunity to work has never left me. I still believe wholeheartedly that the ability to work is one of the biggest blessings we are given.

Many brilliant young founders, while they're fundraising, ask venture capitalists for feedback on their go-to-market strategies or business models. Asking questions is great, but then they slip up:

instead of hearing the answers, they get defensive and start to argue the merit of their original approach. They're worried that, in the face of any challenge, they need to prove their intelligence. In fact, the opposite is true: when someone takes the time to give you feedback, it is because they think you are worthy of it.

Humility doesn't imply lack of self-confidence—in fact, it suggests the opposite. Marc Benioff, founder and CEO of Salesforce, whose board I served on for more than six years, is a great example. His persona has always been highly self-assured, and he's known as someone who marches to the beat of his own drum. Yet when we worked closely together on the various challenges that Salesforce faced in those early years, he consistently sought my input and took my feedback and advice with an open and willing mind. Because he was self-assured, he never felt the need to be defensive. Marc was always a thoughtful listener who knew that hearing different ideas from those he trusted would make him a better CEO and leader.

There's another benefit that comes with humility: the willingness to be flexible and alter course when you hit a roadblock. Again, it's that ability to flow like water. There are many routes to any given destination, but not everyone is prepared to travel one that looks different from the one they originally plotted.

Earlier I mentioned failing to find investors for my first startup, which was going to be the world's first commercial Internet Service Provider (ISP). At the time Internet usage was strictly noncommercial and limited to academic institutions, government agencies, and research organizations. Several universities around the country provided Internet access. My cofounder, Dan Lynch, and I wanted to expand Internet access to the rest of the world, and specifically, to use the Internet to conduct commerce by partnering with universities to create a for-profit company. It was a revolutionary concept, to use the Internet for business, and it had very few fans.

For two years we met with universities, trying to buy their Internet access entities. We finally negotiated a deal with Stanford University's BarrNet, which we would make the nucleus of our ISP. We thought our plan was brilliant and the execution completely manageable. All we needed was the cash to pay for the acquisition of BarrNet. Besides our relationship with Eric Schmidt, we even had the blessing of the likes of Vint Cerf, considered by many to be the father of the Internet.

We visited every venture capitalist in town, pitching our idea that the Internet was the future of commerce. In hindsight, using the Internet for business sounds like a no-brainer. We do it every day. At the time, though, everybody thought it was crazy. They all turned us down.

However, while investors may have thought we were crazy, fellow entrepreneurs didn't. There was an entity called UUNet in Reston, Virginia, that was working on the same goal. We made an agreement to partner with them, and Dan and I folded all our work into their efforts. That meant giving up our founder status, but we both saw immediately that this would allow us to capitalize on all the work we had done and to move forward. I worked long, strenuous hours with UUNet for a year, taking home no paycheck. My husband was beginning to doubt my sanity for continuing to work so hard for no pay.

"I'm getting paid in stock because the company doesn't have much cash, but believe me, this will pay off," I told him.

Sure enough, when UUNet went public in 1994 and became the largest commercial ISP of its day, serving large enterprises across the country, my considerable holdings translated into my first real payday.

When no one would invest in us, Dan and I could have just given up and turned sour, calling our efforts a waste, a loss, or a failure. Instead, we put aside our egos and thought pragmatically about how to find a useful home for all the work we had done and move forward in a productive, constructive way. I had the confidence to know that although I was not the company's original founder, I had made a significant contribution and got rewarded for it.

WHEN IT'S TIME
TO SHOOT THE RAPIDS

The story that people always ask for—how I became the first investor of Salesforce—is actually a pretty good one. Marc Benioff and I met during my CyberCash days at that AGENDA conference where I was a panelist. Marc and I quickly became friends, and shortly thereafter, business associates when Oracle, where he worked, decided to use our payments system; he was our champion there. Later, when I joined U.S. Venture Partners (USVP) and became a venture capitalist, Marc and I would consult each other on ideas from time to time, and we collaborated on several investments. One day Marc invited me to the Peninsula Golf Club in Burlingame, California, to get my take on a new idea.

Silicon Valley, then as now, is full of bright minds churning away. Even so, I passed on most of the ideas I heard pitches for as a venture capitalist. What every investor is looking for is an idea that is more than a viable company; investors are hungry to invest in businesses that can redefine industries and reshape how business is done.

That day at the club Marc told me about his idea for a new way to provide the software that large enterprises use to communicate with customers to a new market. Immediately I felt it deep down: this idea was in that rare group.

At the time the enterprise business software that allowed companies to maintain customer data was available only to the giant players who had multimillion-dollar technology budgets to buy licenses and then spend millions more to implement the software, a process that was so complicated that there was an entire industry of consulting firms dedicated to it.

What if, Marc proposed, you radically simplified the software and gave the most useful 20 percent of the existing functionality to small and midsize businesses for a tiny fraction of the price tag? Instead of selling licenses and having clients implement the software in their own systems, you would offer the software as a subscription, accessible via the Internet. Customers would pay only for what they used, and they would be up and running immediately without any need for costly and long integration.

"So what do you think?" Marc asked me.

I didn't hesitate.

"That's not just a good idea," I told him. "It's a *phenomenal* idea." I rattled off the reasons why. Here was an underserved small and midsize enterprise market with clear demand for customer management tools but unable to afford the million-dollar-plus price tag of the existing software solution. More importantly, I saw that the agility made possible by this new subscription delivery method was the future of the software business, which had always struggled with upgrades and versions. Moving away from the clunky old licensing model would allow for incredible innovation and value generation.

Then I said exactly what every entrepreneur hopes to hear: "I'm going to invest my own money. But more than that, I'm going to support you and help you do whatever it takes to make you successful. I'm in it with you all the way."

I believed in Marc, and the vision he spelled out coincided exactly with where I thought enterprise software technology had to move. I gave Marc a few moments to take this all in, then I got to business.

"Okay, now what's next? What do we need to make this happen?"

Marc told me that to move forward, we needed to convince Left Coast Software, the three-man team of the Valley's best engineers, to commit to our project. "They've been skeptical about the value," he told me. "I can't get them all to buy in."

We decided that as the company's newly minted first investor, I should speak directly with Parker Harris, leader of the team. Later that afternoon I got on the phone with Parker. While already committed to joining Marc, Parker was concerned about the risk of losing out to potential competitors. He asked what our competitive advantage would be. "None! No barriers to entry either," I told him. "So what? Anyone can do almost anything. Competitors are inevitable. But we'll do it right, and we'll do it big. What we need is the guts to go for it in a big way."

I took a breath, then made my final pitch.

"If we commit fully, move fast, and execute better than everyone else, no one can outdo us."

Following the call I felt confident that the entire Left Coast Software team would sign up for the mission, and they soon did.

TOSS YOUR LIFE PRESERVER

Sustaining self-belief is the ultimate challenge for so many entrepreneurs, particularly women. With all the smart competition out there, it seems presumptuous to think that you will be the one who wins the race. And taking the risk of committing yourself 100 percent? That can just seem foolish.

We all need a push every so often—even Marc, one of the most self-driven individuals I know. By July 1999 we had Parker Harris, Frank Dominguez, and Dave Mollenoff working in a one-bedroom apartment next to Marc's home on Telegraph Hill. We had made several other full-time hires. Friends would come by regularly to brainstorm. We all sat on the floor in front of the prototype and spent endless hours discussing what should be included and how the user interface should be laid out.

Traditionally software had been developed in total secrecy until its public launch. We threw that out in favor of getting feedback from as many people as we possibly could, which proved to be a major strength. Unlike others, we were able to define and redefine the product as we went. *Simple, intuitive, and fast* was our approach.

Soon we needed to raise more money. My own partners at USVP turned us down. They decided to place their bet on the established player in the category, Siebel Systems, which was launching a product called Sales.com to compete with us directly. It was awkward, but I wasn't going to leave Salesforce. I was already invested, both financially and emotionally.

After my firm passed, I presented Salesforce to many of my venture capital friends, but they also doubted our vision. They didn't believe a hosted delivery model could work because it required companies to hand over their most precious jewels—high-security customer and sales data—to Salesforce, to be stored in the cloud instead of on-site.

Because venture capital wasn't coming through, we continued to meet with private investors. One meeting went particularly well, and as we walked out, both Marc and I felt optimistic we might finally have a backer.

But there was one thing that concerned me: Marc had not yet cut the cord from Oracle. He had a very satisfying and secure role there as well as a real friend and mentor in his boss, Larry Ellison. Even though Marc had taken a leave of absence to spend all his time on Salesforce, I felt strongly that it was time for him to show full commitment. Leaving Oracle would prove to our prospective investor—and hopefully, future ones—that he was "all in" and not hedging his bet.

"It is time for you to be a full-time entrepreneur," I said to Marc, who towered over me as we waited to cross a busy San Francisco street corner. (Marc is six-foot-five to my five-foot-seven.)

If he didn't commit fully, our growth would be limited. Our fundraising would continue to be challenged, and it would be difficult to hire the best employees, who might see Marc's connection to Oracle as a hesitation to commit to Salesforce. True leaders show everyone that they believe 100 percent in their vision and are taking the same risk they are asking of their investors and their employees.

At first I remember him looking at me like, *Really? This is working. Why rock the boat?* I explained my reasoning, and he agreed that it was the right thing to do. Salesforce.com became Marc's only job.

Not long after, the investor we had met with that day committed $5 million.

Almost any entrepreneur or anyone advocating for themselves against the odds will have crucible moments such as that one. There are ways to hedge risk, but you can't hedge your commitment. You need to believe, and you need to find that belief within yourself—most of the time no one is going to give it to you. In fact, plenty of people will try to take it away.

What did Marc do on his first day of being a full-time Salesforce employee? He went to look for a new space for the company because our employees now had spilled out of the next-door apartment into his house. The new space was the Rincon Center, and it was enormous. At that time Salesforce was ten people. When Parker saw it he famously shook his head and declared, "Eight thousand square feet? That's way too much space. We'll never use it all!"

A year later we had outgrown the place and moved to One Market. Today the new Salesforce Tower is on its way to being the largest building west of the Mississippi.

THE URGENCY AND FEAR
OF TRUE COMMITMENT

My own first "crucible" commitment—and by no means my last—came well before I had ever risked my time or money launching a company. It involved higher stakes than I have ever faced since. It was when, at age seventeen, I chose to leave my parents—and my entire life, as I had known it—to start my higher education in the United States. I actually had to make the decision two different times: first, as a freshman, and then again after my sophomore year, when continuing my education at Stanford appeared to be a permanent commitment to life in the States.

Business books rarely discuss one of the most difficult aspects of taking a risk: you are making the decision for more than yourself. The effects can't help but spill over to your loved ones, your family, and your friends. They may or may not approve, and it's up to you to look inside and decide what to do with your "wild and precious life," in the words of the poet Mary Oliver.

My father always told me I could do anything in life, as long as I clearly evaluated all the costs associated with my chosen path and was prepared to pay the complete price. He instilled in me a love for adventure, but he was clear that I needed to do it with full awareness of the risks.

"Anyone can take a risk by shutting their eyes," he used to say. "The trick is taking a risk with eyes wide open. "

Even though at an early age I had made the decision to go to college in the United States, it was all very abstract until my senior year of high school, when the reality of the consequences started to become clear. I had attended the same all-girls junior high and high school and had spent seven years with the same fifty-five young women. They were more than my friends—they were my sisters. Most of them would continue together to universities in Istanbul. And I would be leaving my boyfriend behind, whom I cherished.

I grew up in a neighborhood called Moda, where almost every shop owner had known me since I was born. They had watched me transform from a chubby little girl into the young swan that I was at seventeen. I had spent my summer days on the Princes Islands in the Sea of Marmara, where there were no cars allowed and donkeys were our four-wheel-drive vehicles. I loved Turkey and all its quirks. I loved my mysterious ancient city of Istanbul, with its crooked streets, and I loved Turkish literature and music; in short, I loved my homeland.

As I considered leaving all this, melancholy set in. I started getting homesick before even buying a plane ticket. When I thought of my future in America, I could barely draw in one detail. It was a big, bright blank. The more I thought—the wider I opened my eyes—the more I got cold feet.

And then I turned my attention to the most difficult challenge: leaving my parents behind. My sister had left Turkey for middle school, and I had seen how much my mother suffered from having her far away. Our little family celebrated each letter that arrived from my sister as if it were a winning lottery ticket. Now that she was in and out of the country as a flight attendant, her short periods away were deeply felt. Unlike her, though, I would be leaving for nine months, not just one or two weeks, and I would be going to the other side of the world—a place my parents had never even been to. The only person my father "knew" from Chicago was Al Capone. He really didn't want his little girl to venture so far west for college—to the City of Gangsters, no less. My father's formal education had ended at fifth grade, the saddest day of his life he used to say, when he had to quit school to make money to support his family. He desperately wanted me to continue my studies; he just didn't want it to be a world away.

Fear ran through my whole body, as I contemplated how my parents would fare without me. I finally began to understand that the gravity of my decision was not only a personal one, but also one that involved all my loved ones. I was not the only person who would pay a price for venturing into the unknown, but I would be risking the happiness of those I cared for most. This weighed heavy on my heart.

As my departure day ticked close, I had several conversations with my father about the emotional price they would be paying for my choice. He told me it had to be my decision; I had to own it. And I did. I made the final commitment to follow through on my dream. Yes, the risks were great and the outcome was unknowable—but I could feel in myself that if I stepped back from the dream, I would find only misery, and I would eventually make others miserable, too. I also couldn't squelch the feeling that I had more to offer the world than I could make happen from the place of my birth, no matter how much I loved it.

And so, dressed in my most beautiful clothes, I flew away to America, sure that I had achieved my father's standard of opening my eyes wide enough to consider every outcome. The truth was that I had completely underestimated the price my parents would later bear for my decision. But this is the reality of taking a risk. I believe I would make the same decision again today. I *must* believe it, if I'm to continue to take the big leaps that make life rich.

A true entrepreneur has wide capacity in her heart for adventure and learning—but none at all for regret.

2

Be the Boss of
Your Own Career

Powered-UP women are the bosses of their own careers. This holds whether you work for a company or run your own business. No one is more influential to your own success than you. Don't like the rules of the game? It's up to you to rewrite them. People talk a lot about "being in the moment," but I don't think that applies well to career management if you want to keep moving forward. Instead, once you know what you want, find ways to live in that future right away, whatever your job description. Take on new responsibilities before those responsibilities are given to you. Ask for the promotion before it is offered, maybe even before you deserve it. Take the giant step forward before you have all the terrain mapped. Be the boss.

Take someone like Clara Shih. She's only thirty-five years old and is the CEO of her own company, Hearsay, which provides software for financial advisers to better leverage social media, mobile, and digital and more efficiently build relationships with their clients. She's also a board member at Starbucks, the youngest in the company's history. The way you get that far that fast is by being your own boss, which means not letting your job title define or limit what you have to offer.

That was Clara's approach even as a summer intern at Microsoft during her undergraduate years at Stanford. She didn't limit herself to classic intern "grunt work"; instead she left a legacy. She became the intern who wrote the original RSS feature for Outlook, one of Microsoft's most important products.

At the time, blogs were rising in influence as social networks and news providers. RSS feeds were created to allow people to read all their blogs in one place instead of needing to visit each website. So she told her older colleagues and bosses that "Outlook is going to need an RSS feed," a way to let people read their blogs without leaving their email program. But her higher-ups weren't blog readers yet themselves, so they didn't get it. Instead of letting the issue drop, however, Clara volunteered to do it herself.

"I didn't know how RSS worked," says Clara, "but nobody on my team knew how it worked either. It was new. I was at no greater disadvantage than anyone else. Even though I was an intern, we were on even footing."

It took several all-nighters in the final two weeks of her internship, but when she left she handed off the code. To this day, despite the diminishing influence of RSS, you can find her feature—many versions later—in Outlook.

In 2006 Clara joined Salesforce as a founding product marketer on the AppExchange, which is where I met her. Again she noticed an opportunity: Facebook, then still new, could be an incredible tool for salespeople. And again her bosses were not sure of the value. So she built the app FaceForce on her own, during nights and weekends, and when she was ready we released it. It went viral, and its success changed not just our business but also her life. Prentice Hall approached her to write a book about Facebook as a business tool, and that book deal led to a relationship with Sheryl Sandberg, who connected Clara to her first investor. Six years and $51 million in venture funding later, Hearsay is strong and growing, and Clara has published her second book. She told me, "At Microsoft and Salesforce I didn't set out to be entrepreneurial. I actually wanted the big company to do it. I didn't feel entitled to do it. I thought, *RSS is a big deal. Facebook is a big deal. Someone who is much more senior and has much more experience than me ought to be doing this.* But I spoke up, and when people dismissed it as a dumb idea, I refused to believe them, and I just did it myself."

An entrepreneur—whether within a company or independent—creates opportunities for herself. It takes courage, but on the flip side you've got one assurance: no one else has ever done what you're suggesting, so you're as qualified as anyone else. In fact, you're more qualified. You're the one who spotted a need and defined a solution. You can *own* that.

BE PREPARED TO ZIG AND ZAG

Most conventional career advice is useless to tech aspirants. The worn-out idea that you should set a long-term goal and then create a map to it is overwhelming in any context but almost ludicrous in the world of technology. In five years an industry that doesn't exist today might hold your dream job.

Like many people who have founded companies, I didn't set out with that as a goal. My first job, at Advanced Micro Devices (AMD), was a very traditional corporate experience. We were number two in the chip space. Our main competitor, Intel, was known for having the more innovative products, but we kept pace due to quick execution and a stellar sales and marketing organization. But it always seemed to me that the really cool stuff in technology and even in microprocessors was happening somewhere else.

Still, I was fortunate to have a great boss—the one who applauded my "delicious eff-you attitude"—who helped me make my time at AMD valuable. Even though he was the head of applications engineering, he encouraged me to shift from product design to product management, where the money was better and I could put both my technical and people skills to work. Talk about salary transparency: he actually pulled out his paycheck and waved it at me, saying, "Do you really want this to be the most money you ever make?"

Product management in the semiconductor space at the time was a very literal opportunity to sell the future. In fact, it was a job requirement. In order to be successful, a new chip needed to be "designed in" to the computers that would be produced three full years down the line. (This is still the case, but the cycle is now much shorter.) The semiconductor product manager's job was to get engineers at computer and communications systems companies, the future buyers, committed to including their company's chip in a next-generation design. Meanwhile all they've got to work with is engineering and functional specs because the product itself doesn't yet exist. Selling the future became a skill that would later help me attract investors and partners to my startups—I knew how to convey a vision of something big, even if it was in the distance.

Meanwhile AMD was a sprawling company with many divisions, departments, and leaders intent on defending their turf. You had to be careful not to step on anyone's toes. After a couple of years there I wanted to be at a smaller company where I'd have more latitude to be my own boss and stray from my job description. I researched the field and identified a "hot" startup, Fortune Systems, where I interviewed and accepted a job that made me one of the first few dozen employees.

Fortune Systems made the very first multiuser desktop computer systems running on the UNIX operating system. In true startup style I soon found myself juggling many responsibilities. I managed the UNIX operating system of the new multiuser computer and was responsible for multiple application software packages, including the database from a little startup named Oracle. I also led product marketing campaigns, despite never having had a class in marketing or any experience whatsoever. I had no idea what I was doing and loved every minute of it. I reported to the vice president of marketing, who called me "Flame" because of my wild auburn hair and taught me a lot, despite the total lack of formal training.

Fortune was on a rocket ship. The first quarter that we shipped our UNIX-based computer systems we booked $20 million in revenue. Our hot startup went public during our second quarter of product shipment, the seventh-largest IPO in the history of the United States.

But only three months later our "hot" startup was struggling. (See how fast things can change?) Our stellar revenue figures all came from unloading the product onto distribution partners, who weren't finding enough end-user customers and were asking to make returns. Seeing the writing on the wall, I left the company and shifted into strategic management consulting at Booz Allen, where I knew I'd get more structured training and a broad business background. It was a great MBA that I did not need to pay for—they paid me! During my years there I learned all the business school basics, such as how to analyze market size and potential, read and create financial statements, make pro-forma projections, conduct user market research, and more.

Booz brought me in with the promise that I'd work with technology clients on next-generation product strategies, but I ended up working mostly with consumer companies. My most memorable project was when I spent several months defining and designing features for new cruise ships. Having never stepped foot on one, I was uniquely unqualified, so I was immediately sent on a "product appreciation trip"—that is, a cruise. I could not believe my good fortune. I spent the next several months running focus groups on Viking, Norwegian, and Royal Caribbean ships. (If you have ever enjoyed a private balcony or a running track on a ship, you've got our team to thank.)

Riding cruise ships was great cocktail fodder (not to mention a crash course in user research and usability testing), but I missed working with technology companies and didn't want everything I had learned so far to be obsolete by the time I stepped back in. So I left Booz to start my own technology-focused consulting firm. I had one partner in the United States, two in Europe, and a team who grew depending on what work we'd sold. The company operated successfully until we were burglarized twice, two weeks apart. All our computers were stolen. The second time we lost our replacement computers, which contained all our research and our final project report for our biggest client. (In the chaos after the first theft we hadn't backed anything up.) We lost the client and our cash flow. We had to let our staff go and give up our lease. It was devastating.

I wanted to get out of consulting and back into high tech. I spent the next months interviewing, but I had been out of the game long enough that the people interviewing me—my future bosses—were not only younger than me but also had lesser qualifications. It was at that point that I started to realize that if I was going to get back into tech without making a leap backward, I needed to create something myself. Not long after, I stepped fully into foundership and found my rhythm. So can you be a successful entrepreneur with a career that zigzags wildly, without a five-year plan? Absolutely.

Wunderkind like Mark Zuckerberg along with the abbreviated "140-character" nature of communication in the social era have ratcheted up the pressure on young people today to succeed quickly. That's the opinion of Debby Hopkins, the chief innovation officer at Citi and CEO of Citi Ventures. "You cannot build your career by speaking only in headlines," says Debby. "You have to take the time to peel back every layer of a business problem to fully understand it and offer a solution."

Debby's own professional zigzag suggests a powerful means to develop that onion-peeling ability. Her thirty-five-year career spans five industries, four of which were in manufacturing. Even though people have traditionally focused on moving forward and up in one industry, she has found that the breadth of experience gained by transitioning her knowledge to new contexts made her a much more conscientious and creative thinker and problem solver.

Debby's first job was in Ford's tractor division, where she was the only woman. You wouldn't think that her work there would offer much insight to the problems she's solving in her work today at

Citibank, but she says the opposite is true. At Ford she worked with engineers to help price special-order tractors. They taught her systems thinking: not just knowing how every bolt worked but also how it affected the rest of the machine. "I have used that systems thinking throughout my career," she says. "In the mobile social world, where you have to think of the user's complete experience, every detail and every step adds to defining the whole system." Her goal at Citibank as the chief innovation officer has been to focus on the whole consumer experience, moving the bank away from looking at the business as a series of consumer transactions. In other words, it's still about the tractor, not just the bolts.

While you're zigzagging through your own career, allow yourself to try different models—old and new companies, established firms and startups. Rigid, abstract ideas about your future can lead you to miss opportunities that come your way. The talented programmer and cofounder of Beluga, Lucy Zhang, told me that she had learned that lesson during her early days at Google. Her first project at the company was for a Google Adwords product. "I was idealistic," she told me. "I had this notion from college that my passion was machine learning. So I went to Google News, where I had friends and there were more machine learning projects."

Only years later did she realize what a great situation she had left behind at Adwords, the company's major revenue generator. First, it was a high-impact position offering visibility within the company. And second, she had a great mentor in her tech lead, who was always active in making sure she was recognized for her work.

She stayed at Google News for three years not because she loved it but because she "felt inertia." Her energy picked back up when she started learning iOS development independently, eventually leading to the very difficult decision to leave Google. Ultimately Lucy joined up with two other ex-Googlers to create the messaging app Beluga, which they sold to Facebook just a few months after launching in 2011. Leaving Google had turned out to be the right decision. She now works at Facebook.

THE CASE FOR GOING CORPORATE

Foundership gets a lot of attention these days. People now see starting their own company as the fast path to glory, the single-best way for bold, creative genius to flourish. Meanwhile corporate careers are portrayed as the home of cogs and cubicles. But that thinking is unnecessarily zero-sum. There are real upsides to joining a company. Although there are more politics to being your own boss in a large, established corporation, the resources you have at your disposal when you do take initiative are incomparable. There's also that little detail of a reliable paycheck.

Clearly you don't need to be a founder or even to work for a young, high-growth company to have a career exploring the cutting edge in technology. Many of the women I've spoken to agree that it can actually be a mistake to focus too narrowly on foundership as a goal. Instead, find great people and consistently bigger problems to solve. Michelle Zatlyn, the cofounder and COO at Cloudflare, put it well: "Find a problem that you really care about, that you'd be really proud of solving, and find the best way to go do that. If you can be the person who starts that team to do that, great, but if there's already a team doing it really well, go join them."

Michelle went to business school with the intention of finding a high-growth company to join after she left. "I wanted to find a Google before it was Google or a Starbucks before it was Starbucks," she told me. But in her last semester at Harvard her focus shifted when she joined classmate Matthew Prince on a school project to develop a business plan. The final deliverable would be to pitch the plan at a university-wide competition.

"I never said, 'I'm starting a company.' I got involved because I wanted to learn how to pitch," she said. Over the course of the semester the school project grew into a viable business plan for a web security and performance company. Michelle fell more in love with the work every day.

In the meantime she had found her own "Google" when a former classmate offered her a position at LinkedIn. It was everything she had wanted, and yet she wasn't ready to walk away from Cloudflare, which by then had won the business plan competition and gotten an offer to be a part of a venture-capital firm's summer incubator program. It wasn't an easy decision to make, but the summer program helped Michelle see the startup route as a credible option. Ultimately she decided she had to see what she could do with Cloudflare. "You're making the biggest mistake of your life," her friend at LinkedIn told her when she turned him down. "I was not confident at all that it was the right choice," Michelle told me. That was the summer of 2009.

Fast-forward to today, and even though LinkedIn's rise has been as meteoric as she expected, Michelle no longer doubts that she made the right call. Cloudflare is a massive success in its own right. Today 425 people work at Cloudflare, with offices in San Francisco, California; Austin, Texas; Champaign, Illinois; Boston, Massachusetts; Washington, DC, London, and Singapore. In 2014 Cloudflare protected a company against the world's largest-ever-recorded distributed denial-of-service attack, used by hackers to shut websites down. Today the company runs one of the world's largest networks that powers more than 10 trillion requests per month, which is

GOING FAST STARTS WITH SLOW

In the new economy time is always short. People are impatient to see results from your crazy new idea, and competition is always breathing down your back. Many intra- and entrepreneurs feeling this pressure make the mistake of diving too fast into execution. It costs a lot more time and money to fix something after it has been built than to take the time to get it right the first time. Regardless of what the product or service that you are offering is, invest thoughtful time upfront. Let simplicity be the guiding principle that keeps you from getting overly bogged down. Then, once you've mapped the solution, go fast to execute.

nearly 10 percent of all Internet requests for more than 2.5 billion people worldwide.

"We've really taken this idea that started way back on the school campus and turned it into a real company with real customers, four million customers, and are delivering on our promise," she says with well-earned pride.

It's smart to spend at least some time working for a big company, particularly early in your career, regardless of whether you see that as your final destination. Sonja Perkins is a veteran venture capitalist who spent most of her career at Menlo Ventures and was ranked among the Top 100 Most Powerful People in Global Finance by *Worth* magazine in 2015. She is troubled by the recent trend that idealizes founding a company at a young age. "Kids in high school are having business plan contests and people are dropping out of Stanford so they can become entrepreneurs. To me it means, 'I don't want to have a boss,'" she says. "I always tell young people entrepreneurs are born and not bred. Unless they have an insatiable desire to solve an unmet problem, their focus should be on getting a great education and finding the smartest people at the best companies they can to work with. With a great foundation, they can truly do whatever they want later."

Sonja credits the first three years of her career at TA Associates, working for the legendary Kevin Landry, with her future success. She spent every day cold-calling and meeting "pretty much all of the software companies in the United States that had the potential to be interesting." She identified more than a few that turned out to be great investments for the firm, including McAfee Associates, OnTrack, and Artisoft. She loved the job, but after three years she left, having decided early on that she wanted to become a partner at a venture-capital firm. At the time that meant going to a top business school. She chose Harvard but felt that TA Associates was her best education. She reflects, "Without working at TA those three years, I would have never been able to have been a partner at Menlo Ventures for twenty years. I would not have had the foundation needed to succeed. Kevin Landry was the best—he was honorable, wanted to win, and trusted his people. So were all the people at TA."

Leah Busque is the founder of the flexible-workforce company TaskRabbit. She started the company in her apartment after wishing she had someone to pick up some food for her dog. Since then she has expanded it worldwide, with nearly $50 million in venture funding, revolutionizing the way people work. *Fast Company* has named her one of the 100 Most Creative People in Business. With this visionary's bio, you might be surprised to learn that Leah spent eight years as a programmer at IBM. The buttoned-up corporate process there meant that you couldn't check in code "if you weren't

100 percent sure it was going to work." The discipline and work ethic she acquired at IBM set her bar for quality high, helping her to develop TaskRabbit into a top-rated consumer service in which punctuality and service quality are paramount.

Julie Wainwright, founder of the luxury consignment business TheRealReal.com, also credits her time as an employee with foundational learning. After graduating from Purdue, she talked herself into a brand-management position at Clorox that was usually reserved for business school graduates. "I told them that they didn't have to pay me as much as an MBA, so they should give me a shot," she told me.

After three years she had a strong foundation in profit and loss, strategy, and marketing management. But she also knew she didn't want to stay: "There were no women in executive positions except in HR." Her next job was at Software Publishing Corp., one of the first personal productivity software companies. It not only honed her skills; it also gave her a startup-like experience within a larger company. "I went over to Europe to set up all international distribution," she told me. "It was me and another guy, and the guy got fired. He had been my boss. They go, 'Can you handle it?' I go, 'Yeah, I think I've got this.' I had to do the business plan. I had to do the work. I had to deliver the results. Talk about focusing me."

The point is that independence isn't always the best way to power UP. Having an organization behind you can provide opportunities, learning, and rigor.

INTRAPRENEURSHIP, OR HOW TO MOVE A MOUNTAIN

One of the most successful entrepreneurs I know—really, one of the idols whom I have always looked up to—is actually an intrapreneur, someone who leads exciting new initiatives inside an established company. Debra Rossi has worked nearly thirty years for one major bank. She is an executive vice president at Wells Fargo and president of the Electronic Transactions Association. Years ago, when she was in credit card acquisitions, she agreed to take a meeting with the husband of her former colleague. He was the CFO of a startup, and he couldn't find a bank that would do its credit card processing.

"Are you making any money?" she asked him.

"No, but we have big investors," he said.

"Well, what's your concept?" she asked.

"Online auctions—beanie babies, mostly."

The idea of going into business with a beanie baby purveyor had sent every other bank running. Not Debra.

Sounds a little high risk, she thought. *May not go anywhere,* she thought. And yet it sounded new and interesting.

"Let's give it a whirl," she said.

The company, of course, was eBay. Business soon exploded, and Debra took the next big step, working with one of eBay's early CEOs, Meg Whitman, to create a company jointly owned by Wells Fargo and eBay that would allow auctioneers to process their transactions online.

These were just a couple of the giant leaps into the future of the Internet's electronic payments that Debra has led at Wells Fargo during her legendary career. Even working within a 165-year-old bank in an extremely conservative, highly regulated industry, she has never been afraid to give tech upstarts a chance. From CyberCash to eBay to PayPal to Square to Stripe, Debra Rossi has been the beacon who has brought innovative companies to the world of payments. When I asked her how she did it, she credited always having a great team as well as support from the top. Her CEO, Dick Kovacevich, encouraged the adoption of new technology, particularly anything that would make banking easier and more flexible for customers. Between his direct support and that of senior management, "We were able to muster the resources," says Rossi.

My own experience working with Debra suggests she is being far too modest, even though her CEO's support was no doubt crucial. Few people are as good at convincing others of her vision as Rossi.

Tanja Omeze is another powered-UP intrapreneur. At companies such as Weight Watchers, Scholastic, Verizon Wireless, and now Amazon, she has created a brand for herself as an innovator. At Verizon, for example, while she was head of digital marketing and business development, she created a super-agile team within a team to help Verizon establish its brand credibility in the mobile app space.

WHEN INNOVATING, ONE SIZE DOES NOT FIT ALL

Courtney Broadus, a key member of the core technology team who built Salesforce, says the key to delivering innovation—whether it's a new feature or a new way of delivering software—is being able to move as quickly as possible at the highest level of quality necessary for the environment you are designing for. That level of quality is different depending on the type of company, who the customer is, and so on. For Salesforce to overturn the enterprise software delivery paradigm, that level of quality had to be high. We hosted our clients' data, their corporate jewels—there was no room for error or a lapse in trust. Meanwhile companies like Amazon or eBay, consumer-facing companies, could afford to take quality risks to maximize speed.

Among the results was a microsite that used data to help customers find great mobile apps, breaking new ground for the company.

Tanja always wanted to be an entrepreneur, but after college she instead took a job offer, thinking she should first get some experience working for others. After she went to business school she launched a startup, but it didn't make it. She returned to corporate America thinking she'd use the time to figure out what to do next. But as her career progressed, she had an epiphany: "At a corporation you have resources—the money—to do some really interesting things. And while it's tough convincing a boss in a company to give you money to do something, it's not nearly as tough as going out and convincing investors to do so."

So she started flexing her entrepreneurial muscles from a corporate foothold. Each time she tried to introduce a new, cutting-edge project, she got a little bit better at setting the conditions for success. Today, as the director of marketing for Amazon Video, she's better positioned to innovate than ever because she's working within a culture that explicitly supports innovators.

Here are a few tips from Tanja on how to excel as an intrapreneur:

▌ DEFINE THE VISION. This is actually the easy part, Tanja says, if you're creative. You're working on the business every day and understand on a deep level what the problems are and what kind of solution might work.

▌ SET EXPECTATIONS. Make it clear that the effort you're leading is a risk. You might fail—but there's enough potential upside that the risk is worthwhile. That way if your experiment fails, you're protected. You established at the start that this was a possible outcome.

▌ **FIND PARTNERS.** There are the official rules in corporate America, and then there are all the ways people can work around the rules if they want to. The key is to find other people who want to work outside the box on exciting, entrepreneurial projects. When you make them your partners, it makes so much more possible.

▌ **MAKE AUTONOMY PART OF THE DEAL.** If you let the broader organization get involved, they'll do what organizations do: require so many sign-offs that progress will get bogged down—and if you do finish, it will be with so many compromises that the idea will get lost.

▌ **SHARE CREDIT.** As the leader of a project you're going to get the win, Tanja says, "so do what's right and give people recognition and credit for the help and the work that they're doing." Sharing credit is a much better way to succeed in organizations than stealing it.

THE BOSS OF
YOUR OWN STORY

At some point being your own boss should lead to becoming an *actual* boss. That means being acknowledged for your accomplishments in the form of not only accolades but also formal titles and authority. There's nothing more hurtful than giving 100 percent to an effort, knowing you played an important role, and failing to be recognized for it. I once had someone try to cut me out of a deal I had brought into the partnership. The situation resolved fairly easily because my contribution was clear to the rest of the team and they were more than willing to advocate on my behalf. But that didn't make the experience any less painful.

Credit isn't usually given—it's taken. You need to ask for it. The challenge is standing up for yourself without becoming one of those obnoxious, aggressively promotional people who seem more worried about getting credit than about getting it right. But the truth is that powered-UP women are not afraid to self-promote. Don't think of it as bragging; think of it as being a thoughtful communicator, someone who can tell a compelling story with herself in an award-winning role. Otherwise, someone else will tell your story for you— and depending on their vantage, their bias, and their agenda, you may or may not feature well in it.

A female technology executive told me she learned this lesson when the company she worked for, a growing startup, decided to create its first head of product. She and a male colleague were both candidates, but she thought she was the shoo-in. Although she deeply respected her colleague, she knew he wasn't ready to be a senior leader. He wasn't particularly attentive to the people side of the business, an area where she put time and attention that she believed made them all more effective. She also had more direct reports than he did.

Then she got devastating news: her boss was planning to offer her colleague the job. She tried to analyze the situation through his eyes: Why couldn't he see what seemed obvious to her? She started thinking about how her performance had been measured in the past and suddenly realized something: they had no existing metrics to measure the very management skills that made her the superior candidate, things like creating the conditions and relationships that lead to productivity, removing underperforming talent promptly (something she found incredibly stressful but did anyway), and making great new hires and integrating them within the team. Aside from this, her boss wasn't a hands-on manager and had a lot to juggle. All he knew about product thus far was that things were working; he had no view on why.

At that moment she realized that whatever role gender was playing in this situation, she had made a major mistake in managing her career. She had always focused on doing her work, believing excellence would be recognized and she would be rewarded with authority. When the company was smaller, that had worked out just fine. But now, she realized, as the company's growth created new opportunities, it was up to her to articulate her own value.

"It took me a while to back into metrics," she told me, "because these were things that were hard to articulate. I knew that I was really sacrificing a lot to be a good leader, and I thought, *How do I show that?*" The most important metric she landed on was the retention rate on her team: she had zero voluntary turnover, which translated into major savings and productivity gains for the company. Meanwhile she also had higher involuntary turnover—in other words, she was firing more people than other managers, actively pruning her team to keep standards high.

Now she felt she had a clear, concrete argument for why she—not her colleague—should be promoted. She asked for a meeting with her boss and campaigned for herself with passion. She also outlined where things would suffer with her colleague in charge. Her boss listened, thought about it, and agreed: the decision had been made too hastily, without real consideration of what the role would require. She should be the new head of product, not her colleague. The promotion became one of the most important of her career, putting her on track to the C-suite. If you want to be the one who gets those choice promotions, you need to create opportunities to share your story and do it in the language of your business: How is your work contributing unique value?

WHEN IN DOUBT, DO WITHOUT

One of the mistakes I have made over and over again in my career is waiting too long to fire someone who is an obvious misfit for the job. It is hard to let someone go who is doing only 50 percent of the job because when they are gone even the 50 percent that they are doing will not get done. So instead, we naturally hang on to the underperformers, worried that we may be much worse off without them.

My advice, when in doubt, do without. (Or, more crudely put, better a hole than an *&$hole. No matter how brilliant, someone who is a true jerk ruins the place for everyone else.) Ask under-performers to leave if you have given them a chance and they have not been able to improve their performance. Once they are gone, as a manager, you will be a lot more motivated to bring in better talent who will satisfy your job requirements.

The way I managed my own career offers a second practice to help you shape what you might call the "historical record" of your performance at work: ask for feedback. I make a point to ask those I'm working with How am I doing? What can I do better? Then I document their responses, especially if they are positive. The easiest way to do this is to use the company's preferred communication, be it email or any sort of messaging. I might say, "Hey, Joe, thank you so much for your positive comments on my presentation and the way I handled the meetings. They really motivated me, so thank you for that." I summarize what they said and thank them for the feedback.

This exchange created a written trail of the contributions I made and people's experience working with me. I never had to wonder what other people thought or where I fit in the bigger picture. If there was a gap between what I believed I was contributing and what I was actually contributing, I could get on top of it right away. And whenever I was in a situation where I needed to negotiate credit, I had incredible leverage and confidence. I didn't need to rely only on my own sense of self or my memory to make my case; I had a folder of my colleagues' testimonials. If my boss said, "You're terrible at managing meetings," I could turn to my folder and say, "But look, here's Joe talking about the fantastic job I did to keep us moving." Actually, I don't think I ever needed to share what was in that folder. It served its purpose by protecting me from creeping self-doubt so I could stand up for myself when I needed to. Data always trumps opinion, so preparing for one-on-ones or reviews with data will always empower you.

Here's what you need to be prepared for with the feedback approach: *it won't always be positive.* And that's what makes this approach particularly effective. Not only are you creating a record of your contributions; you're also constantly getting the information you need to improve what you have to offer. This isn't only about a paper (or electronic) trail; it's ongoing development feedback that you should take very seriously. Your boss will appreciate how well you accept negative feedback, and you'll be a piece of cake to manage.

Asking for feedback once opened my eyes to an embarrassing blind spot that I never would have seen myself. When we started a bicoastal company, with East and West Coast offices, I got into the habit of starting my day at the San Francisco office at 5 a.m. I loved beating my East Coast colleagues to their desks. I'd spend that first, quiet hour downing coffee while knocking out to-dos, which often resulted in creating a million tasks for my team. By the time they showed up I was running a mile a minute, short and snappy from all the caffeine. I'd shower them with demands, expecting gratitude for all I did to kick-start their day and keep things rolling along efficiently and productively.

As you might guess, they weren't grateful. They dreaded "morning Magdalena"—and they told me pretty candidly when I finally asked. Their feedback made me realize that I had to tone it down. I limited myself to one cup of coffee and gave people time to settle in and start their workday on their own terms. If not for their candid feedback, I would still be buzzing in the morning to this day.

Some of the most talented women I know are the most anxious about hearing feedback. That had always puzzled me, but my friend Gina Bianchini, founder of create-your-own-mobile-network company Mighty Networks, recently helped me understand why: "I hold myself to very high standards. Early in my career that made me afraid of feedback," she says. "I wouldn't say I didn't want it, but I didn't make it particularly safe for others to give it to me. Especially as a woman, you have to make it safe and then you have to ask."

Conscientiously getting, recording, and acting on feedback has one more benefit: it shows everyone that you work with that you're proactively trying to be the best you can be. You're responsible and assertive and not too proud to admit there are areas where you can improve. That's the kind of team member everyone goes out of their way to help—and however assertive you are, it's always good to have people to call on to defend or strengthen your case.

EARN A BOSS'S PAYCHECK

My career has never been about money. And yet as an immigrant who came to this country with very little, I tend to recognize its importance. Money is power. At the end of the day the one with the most money is the absolute boss—even CEOs are hired and fired by their investors. When Sonja Perkins and I started strategizing around creating the women's venture-capital and angel investors group that would later emerge as Broadway Angels, we talked about what the group's goals should be.

Sonja said, "The group's goal is to have fun."

I said, "How about we say the group's goal is to make money, and we'll have fun making it?" We all agreed.

Money is one way to measure the value you're creating. And although it's imperfect and by no means the only way to measure your progress, it's one I've noticed that many women tend to underappreciate or even avoid. Historically our status hasn't been defined by our own bank accounts, so we emphasize other measures of career satisfaction: How much we love our work. Whether we respect our colleagues. Whether we are making a positive difference in the world. These are all noble goals, but they are not in line with what the business world uses to divvy up success and power. If we want success in the business world, we need to speak the language of the business world, which is money. We need to learn the vocabulary of spreadsheets, budgets, financial statements, and yes, salaries. We need to become comfortable speaking in these terms.

Money matters, both to you and to the success of your company, whether you're an employee or a founder. It gives you a competitive advantage. It gives you latitude to make decisions on your own terms. It establishes your position in the market as well as in the professional pecking order. If you are paid less than others for similar work and you know it, your confidence can take a hit, no matter how good you are.

Your first principle: love what you do. Your second principle: make sure you're appropriately rewarded for it. Julie Wainwright told me that her biggest career do-over wish concerned compensation.

"If I could do it again, I would have always asked to see where I was versus other executives. I never did, ever," she told me. Julie is the CEO of a high-growth company with a predominantly female staff, and not one candidate or current employee has ever asked her the question. "Absolutely, I'd give them the answer," she says.

If you don't do your research, an employer may pay you not what you're worth but instead what they can get away with. It happened to Sonja in her first job at TA Associates. When she told her boss she was leaving to go to business school, he offered to double her salary. The offer was meant to flatter and retain her, but it did not. She suddenly realized that for the three years she had worked for the company she had potentially been underpaid. Although she treasured the experience, it was a lesson she never forgot.

Remember when I said in Chapter 1 that selling the future can be the key to success? Negotiating your salary—or, if you're an entrepreneur, the value of your product, service, or company—is one of the purest instances you'll ever encounter of selling the future. The best negotiators don't think in terms of "me vs. them"; they take the lead in cocreating a future that is better for both sides. They present the negotiation in a way that leaves both parties better off. If you can be confident and assertive in sketching out the details of that future picture, you've got an advantage.

I mentioned before that Debra Rossi has succeeded because she's able to see and articulate what the future will look like. It's no surprise that she considers negotiations one of her chief strengths. Over the years she's negotiated tough contracts with many corporate heavyweights, most of them men. "They all know right off that bat when they start negotiating with me that I'm no cream puff," said Debra Rossi. "Whatever we're going to do at the table, we're going to make the right decisions and the right deal for both our companies. It's not going to be easy. But I'm fair. I think anyone would say that."

One of her most famous negotiations was with two women: Meg Whitman, then the CEO of eBay, and Janet Crane, the CEO of Billpoint, the company eBay and Wells Fargo had created together. It was 2001, and Billpoint's chief competitor, PayPal, had grown from a tiny little company to "a real competitive headache." Now Whitman wanted to acquire Janet Crane's competitor. In order to do that, eBay would need to buy out Well Fargo's 35 percent stake in BillPoint, as the agreement between the two companies had been exclusive.

"Janet was a tough negotiator. I was a tough negotiator. But we had mutual respect for one another. Still, it didn't take days—it took months and months and months," said Debra. From hearing stories about Debra's extended time at that and many other negotiating tables, I took away three lessons.

Know Your Power

In the negotiation with eBay Debra was lucky to have great leverage: eBay needed out of its contract if it wanted to attempt to acquire PayPal, which was gradually beating it at the highly lucrative online payments game. "Name your price!" Debra recalls Whitman saying.

Very few negotiations begin with such a candid conversation, which speaks to the level of respect and partnership these two women shared. Transparency was the norm.

Leverage or not, your most potent source of power at the table will come from what you uniquely have to offer. Keep your focus there, not on the factors working against you. eBay, by the way, wasn't immediately successful in buying PayPal, which opted for an

IPO in 2002—and immediately went into business with Rossi at Wells Fargo, which became the financial engine to back the company's transactions. (Later Whitman prevailed, shocking the market by paying $1.5 billion for PayPal. In 2015 PayPal again became independent with a second IPO and now is worth more than eBay. Whitman was no fool.)

Even today PayPal is a Wells Fargo customer—and just like in the early days, the contracts take months to negotiate.

Know Where They're Coming From

There's no success in "my way or the highway." With mutual respect and patience you seek to understand what's really important to each party. In Debra Rossi's case that meant digging into the conflict—reviewing new redlines from the attorneys almost daily—and finding ways to create common ground, again and again. Said Debra, "You figure out new ideas. 'Okay, if you don't want this, what could we do about that? What can we create to compensate for what you're not liking?'"

Make It Bigger Than You

This is the most important piece: What's the bigger, grander shared future you're selling? This helps take ego out of the conversation and shifts everyone to a win-win frame of mind. Working with Meg, "We knew the deal was bigger than both of us. The results for what would happen with our companies was more important than either of us," said Debra.

Later, working with PayPal, Debra's ability to sell then COO Reid Hoffman and the rest of the team on the need for compliance—an

informal but potentially tense negotiation—helped ensure the fledg-
ling company's viability. When the post-IPO PayPal approached
Wells Fargo, the startup was working with a small, obscure bank and
really had no idea how to transition its business from being the Wild
West of payments into a secure, compliant financial transactions
engine.

"What made our partnership so great was that PayPal had no
fear," Debra said. "They were ready to do anything. They had the
speed, and we were the guardian angel saying, 'Wait a minute,'
helping them along so that they could grow compliantly and
securely."

Debra makes it sound easy, but for a fast-moving company like
PayPal, there was nothing more painful than addressing compliance,
the onerous march of creating process and practice in line with
regulation. They were fortunate to be in Debra's capable and
convincing hands. Wells Fargo had the experience to help PayPal
implement compliance with the least burden possible to the
company and to customers.

"I used to say to them, 'I know this is hard for you,' because they
used to complain on the phone saying, 'No, we're not going to do
that. You're kidding,'" said Debra. "I would say, 'Think of it this
way: as hard as it is, we're making you a better company.' Today
PayPal has the best security engine, and I think Wells Fargo
contributed to that in some way. They always tell me that it's not
about the pricing; it's about the relationship we have and how we
helped them grow."

In other words, the overall value Wells Fargo offers PayPal allows
them to command a higher price than their competition. To bring
this back to salary negotiations, you have the upper hand in
negotiation when you can confidently sell the future. Know the fair

market value for your role, but don't rely on it to make your case; instead, sell the other side on the details of your joint future. If you can show them how much brighter and better it is with you than without you, you'll have the power to name your price.

So much about success in your career will come down to something called *locus of control*: Do you believe you're stuck with what you've been offered, or do you believe you have power to change conditions, even in those moments when all seems lost? We're not in control of everything, and there will be moments in every career when that truth cuts sharp. But you'll always be the boss of you. Make sure you give that boss all the power she's worth.

3

You Have More
Power Than You Think

You are a confident capable employee, or even a leader. You bring your best to work every day. In short, you're powered UP. There's little you can't accomplish.

All this power can seem to disappear *in an instant* when a colleague or anyone in a professional context focuses his (or her) attention on what's inside your clothes instead of what's inside your head. Whether it is innuendo or an overt pass, it hurts. Even worse, it may lead to a downward spiral of self-doubt or even shame: *Did I do something to invite this behavior?*

The more powered UP you are, the easier it is to know the answer: *absolutely not.*

My secret source of power, that imaginary armor for those moments when someone reduced me to my skirt, was to cloak myself in what you might call *gravitas.*

Let me give you a snapshot of the culture in which I was operating, in the high-technology world of the 1980s. At twenty-one, fresh out of engineering school, I landed my first job as a product design engineer for the microprocessor maker Advanced Micro Devices (AMD), the chief competitor to Intel. I was the only woman in my division of the company who wasn't in an administrative role other than one much more senior woman in legal who, the few times I came in contact with her, wanted nothing to do with me.

Today the CEO of AMD is a woman. Not so in 1981, when a hard-driving salesman named Jerry Sanders was at the helm. In respects as much Hugh Hefner as Steve Jobs, Jerry drove a white convertible Bentley and had been featured on the cover of a serious business magazine wearing a bathrobe. Actually, I liked the guy—his warm style, sincerity, and willingness to be a very tough competitor. Trouble was, under his leadership propositioning women had become an unofficial part of the sales-training process and perhaps the corporate competitive sport with the highest participation ratio.

I had barely gotten my feet wet at the company when I was invited to my first national sales conference to present my product. I was excited and unsure what to expect.

The conference kick-off was at eight o'clock on a Monday morning. I was a lone woman among hundreds of field sales reps—all men, most of them stereotypical "alpha males"—who had flown in from all over the country to get charged up to sell more AMD semiconductors.

According to the program we were to kick off the week-long conference with an "eye opener." I didn't know what that meant, but I could sense a heated anticipation in the room. These guys were enthusiastic about sales, but it was hard to imagine what could have them so hyped up so early on a Monday.

The stage curtains flew up, and my eyes certainly opened: topless women everywhere! The room erupted in a cacophony of uncensored primate whooping as the choreography became increasingly sexually charged. I had never seen anything like it. I had grown up in Turkey, with its predominantly conservative Muslim culture. Here was the libertine America my father had so worried about and warned me to avoid.

I sat there, viscerally uncomfortable, somewhat panicked: *This is the kick-off of my professional career? This is my company?* This *is what it's going to be for years to come?*

I didn't like how I felt in those moments: powerless. I spent the next few hours passively processing what had happened, unable to concentrate at all on the company sales strategy being presented. Suddenly instead of being engaged, I was painfully self-conscious. But other than a few uneasy eyes briefly cast my way as we left the auditorium, I couldn't see that anyone was acting any differently toward me. Or were they?

In the end it didn't matter because I had come to a clear conclusion in my own mind: I was never, ever going to let anybody make me feel that way again. I was taking back the power to control my own emotions. Gravitas—a combination of your dignity and seriousness—is always in your control.

I soon got my chance to deliver on reclaiming my power more publicly. Two nights later at the same conference there was a pre-dinner show in a cabaret-like setting before we broke for dinner.

The lights dimmed and spotlights went up on multiple topless women who proceeded to delight the crowd by fondling each other. This time I wasn't flustered. Well, I was a little flustered. But I didn't feel powerless at all. This time I had a plan.

When the show finished, everyone broke for dinner. I bee-lined across the room to where Jerry Sanders himself was getting up to leave and pulled him aside. I had not met him before.

I knew I had to play this just right if he was to take me seriously. I was upset, but I wasn't going to let him see it. I put on my best school principal meets Dr. Spock face and looked straight into Jerry's eyes. This was the maiden voyage of a technique I'd come back to again and again in my career.

"You and I need to talk," I said. "I am an engineer at your company, and what just happened was unacceptable to me personally. This show of naked women made me feel like I'm not a respected employee of this company. Is that how you want your newly recruited engineer to feel?" I kept my tone even and unemotional, but I was firm. Jerry needed to understand that as my employer, he was responsible for my well-being. My problem was his problem. And he had just failed me.

Jerry Sanders, hard driving or not, clearly had no idea what to do with me. So he offered the best reparation he could come up with in the moment: "Why don't you sit at my table for dinner, where I will be entertaining our top distributors? I heard you're a very good engineer, and I know they will enjoy the company of a good-looking young woman."

That last comment? I rolled my eyes and let it pass. To him it was the highest of compliments, and I felt I had pushed Jerry Sanders's growth enough for one night. And so it was that a low-level nobody at AMD clinked glasses that night at the VIP table with the company's top business partners.

I used the dinner to push my agenda forward. I wasn't angry and combative; I was pleasant but firm. I didn't rail against topless dancing writ large; instead, I simply made everyone there acutely aware of what it felt like to be me, Magdalena, having to sit there while my colleagues acted like orangutans.

The next day I was the talk of the conference and an instant company celebrity. The sales guys were all talking about my chutzpah, not about microprocessors—nor about naked gaggles of women, for that matter. I felt good that I had communicated my stance not just to the CEO and top management but also, through the grapevine, to most of the attendees of the conference. I dealt with any awkwardness by being friendly, open, and engaging in conversation on topics other than the topless shows. No one asked me what I thought about the shows; they already knew the answer.

And from that day onward naked stage acts were no longer part

> You have more power to protect yourself than you
> might think. This attitude protected me even when
> I was working in an environment that was one step
> up from the Playboy mansion.

of the program—at least, not while I was around. (When I left the company I heard the sales conference reverted to the bawdy house for several more years, offering a pretty fair measure of the durability of patriarchy.)

What I learned at AMD was this: you have more power to protect yourself than you might think. By taking control of your career and your image, the brand that defines who you are, you can effectively communicate your power to the world.

DEVELOPING GRAVITAS

Gravitas can't be developed in a moment; it's something you cultivate all day and every day of your career. When you meet people, in your handshake, in your direct eye contact, in your comfortable smile and sincerity of expression, in the way you walk, your posture, your presence, everything about you says, "I mean business, just like you. I'm serious, just like you. I have power, just like you. I am your equal. In fact, I might even be a little bit better."

Humans are part of the animal kingdom. We smell each other's intentions. So clearly defining your intentions for yourself—"driven to succeed on my professionalism"—puts you in a good position out of the gate. The messaging continues with the way you dress and carries through to your body language. When I meet someone I stand tall and confident, shake their hand firmly, and look them straight in the eye with a smile on my face. At the same time I'm usually very friendly and open, radiating a genuine interest and excitement in meeting a new colleague. My behavior is the same whether I'm meeting a man or a woman.

Recently I was at the home of a friend, and her twenty-one-year-old daughter was there. She told me she was on her way to a professional job interview and asked for some tips on how to answer certain interview questions. I was surprised by her clothing choice. She was wearing an incredibly casual outfit with a short, tight skirt. After I answered her questions I told her my most important tip was that she should change into a more professional-looking outfit.

She was immediately defensive. "Things are different today, Magdalena," she told me, with the forceful wisdom of youth. "You can be who you are at work."

Of course, she's right: things are different today. Young women now assume their right to a space at the table, and that natural confidence and power give them considerable liberty to feel comfortable exhibiting a range of choices in dress and comportment. I celebrate this confidence, but it doesn't eliminate the importance of building an image and a professional brand.

It is wonderful that even in male-dominated fields millennial women generally don't feel the need to do what the legendary founder of Cardyltics, Lynne Laube, and many others did: "Hide all the things that made me uniquely a woman." In Lynne's words, "Early in my career in financial services, I wore pantsuits, I talked about football (I hate football), I made male jokes. And just as important as what I did was what I didn't do. I never used some of the traits that are now my strengths. I hid my empathy. I didn't want to talk about the 'softer' side of a situation, like how customers or employees might react to something. At my company at the time, if you couldn't quantify the impact mathematically, it didn't exist."

Even though I have always enjoyed skirts and pretty shirts, there were many times I found refuge in my office team's unofficial uniform—generic, unremarkable, dark wool pants and button-down shirts. But there were other parts of my femininity I refused to hide. I wore my thick red-auburn hair long and kept it natural, which led to that nickname "Flame." I also stayed away from makeup because I did not have the patience or the time to deal with putting it on and taking it off. In other words, I made my own choices about how to show my femininity. I didn't adhere to anyone else's standard.

While I was growing up my father had hammered into my head that I was like marble. He used to say that marble was beautiful with its own unique patterns; people never painted over it. Looking back on it, I see my hair and makeup choices as reflections of self-confidence, which included my femininity. Having grown up in a culture where serving others was of utmost importance, I shocked the male partners at my venture capital firm by serving coffee or cookies during meetings. Believe me: when we got down to business I could be more vicious than the most vicious guy in the room. But before ripping apart the flaws in their arguments, I'd make sure they had cream. I was raised to be polite. Where I am from, hospitality is a top priority, regardless of one's gender.

Today leaders in high tech and almost every other industry have increasingly emphasized the value of bringing our authentic selves to work. This is a good thing. Your clothes should help you feel comfortable in your own skin. Adopting someone else's uniform can make you feel like an imposter when what you want is the confidence that you bring something special to the table. The business writer Carlye Adler told me what happened when she asked one of her first bosses, a woman, about the dress code. The boss didn't have a simple answer, but she offered, "Back when I worked at the *Wall Street Journal* the most successful reporter wore a green leather skirt every day. Just wear what works for you." That seems to be the spirit of the Silicon Valley hoody clan, after all, though they have a more utilitarian bent.

Sandra Day O'Connor, the first female Supreme Court justice, is one of my heroes. Like all trailblazers, she had to work harder than her colleagues to make it to the bench. I got to meet her once because her son was a classmate at Stanford. Listening to her talk about the challenges she faced, I sensed no hardened attitude, no bitter tone; instead, I saw a highly pragmatic woman who focused on the task at hand yet was never afraid to be soft and loving. In my brief exchange with her she told me that she baked cookies for her staff regularly, which they loved and she believed led to them working harder. She was comfortable with a motherly approach to leadership. Being a nurturer doesn't render you weak or subservient, two adjectives that no one would ever associate with O'Connor.

But let's be honest: society still tries to pigeonhole women, and finding a confident, authentic leadership persona can be fraught. Plenty of tech companies—both when I was coming up in my career and still today—value some women for their minds and others for their appearance. The tradition can be seen in the movie about Facebook, *The Social Network*, or the TV series *Silicon Valley*. Trade show "booth babes" and "marketing hotties" were a thing when the industry was new, and they still are—ask any woman in tech to dispute this. I never worked anyplace where the receptionist wasn't extraordinarily good looking and dressed to broadcast that. I remember once watching as one of these receptionists entered and a ripple of excitement went through the room full of engineers. Once she had exited, one of them said to me, "She may look fantastic, but she probably thinks that a Fast Fourier transform is a race horse." (For nongeeks, a Fast Fourier transform is a numerical algorithm used all the time in engineering.) With his binary thinking, appropriate for a computer engineer, he assumed women were either beautiful and dumb or smart and unattractive.

By and large, individual women today are still shouldering the exhausting work of re-educating these binary thinkers, one at a time. Company leaders in Silicon Valley and elsewhere need to step up and change that, and every woman ought (a big *ought*, which I'll come back to later in the chapter) to feel comfortable in demanding they do. But in the meantime your clothing choices are an immediate tool you can wield to further your goals and shape perception. Ask yourself, *Who do I want to be? What is the brand I am building for myself, and how do my clothes express all that?* Men should ask themselves these questions as well, although their range of choices in this domain are generally more limited.

We each can and will have our own answers, but this conscious evaluation may lead to more nuanced choices than "what feels good." Every working person exists within a culture and has an opportunity to define themselves within that culture with their dress choices. That's pragmatic, and it's the truth. The key is to define what goal you are after and then choose your packaging to bring you closer to that end—consciously, deliberately, authentically, and while having fun with it.

Rachel Maddow touched on this approach to dress in a *Lenny* magazine interview. Writer Grace Dunham asked Maddow whether her journey from radical activist to mainstream MSNBC host had required her to make compromises. Maddow's answer fascinated me: "I don't feel like I have had to invent a fiction about myself or become something that I'm not. I definitely feel like it took me a while to learn the baseline things you have to do if you want people to hear you," said Maddow. "That's why I've had the same haircut for the entire time that I've been on television and that's why I wear literally the same jacket every day. I keep all the clothes I wear on TV in my office on a little hanging rack. My girlfriend calls it all the colors of the German rainbow. Grays, blacks, a slightly greenish gray for the days that I'm feeling particularly festive. I'm not trying to accomplish anything in the way I look other than to be boring enough for people to hear me."

Maddow needs to be able to sit across from everyone from Rick Santorum to Elizabeth Warren and ask pointed questions—an extreme situation for which she's developed a wonderfully minimalist solution. Nevertheless, it's instructive for the rest of us. Some people will want their clothes to be part of their conversation. Some, like Maddow, won't. But we all need to be aware that our appearance does speak to those we work with. You can be sure that Elizabeth Holmes, the CEO of Theranos, whose career had a very fast rise and even a faster fall, didn't start wearing a black turtleneck every day just because it was in her closet. It was a conscious choice that communicated, *Just as Steve Jobs was a cutting-edge leader, so am I.* Her unspoken message was not lost on her early investors and business partners.

One last word on the best attire for your work: wear the clothes that make you feel most powerful, most in control of your environment. What matters more than what others think of your attire is what you think of it. Shortly after we graduated from college, my best friend, Kristi Wagner, transitioned into the computer field, even though she had studied biology and knew nothing about computers. Nevertheless, she would put on her work garb, and her confidence in it made her feel "bitchin'," as she put it. Over time that attitude carried her up on the career ladder. If you feel most powerful in a black dress, wear it. If you feel you need a blazer to feel confident and strong, do that. When you feel powerful and confident inside, you communicate that to the rest of the world. And that is the brand you want to build for yourself: powerful and confident.

SEXUAL HARASSMENT IS A CRIME

Whether the perpetrator is male or female, straight or gay, sexual harassment is wrong. I want to encourage *all* who are on the receiving end of harassment to make formal, public, documented complaints. (I've noticed that as fraught as it is for women to speak openly about sexual harassment—many women declined to be interviewed for this chapter—it is even harder for those men who have lived through it.) Nothing is more powerful than careful, fact-based documentation when it comes to making your case. It gets the subjective interpretation and emotion out of the equation and puts the decision maker—the HR person, the management, the public reading the story or the jury in the courtroom—in a position to draw conclusions on the facts.

I have often wondered why, after years of sexual liberation, we women still stop short of publicly exposing our harassers or making formal complaints. We still, in essence, protect them. With all the tools available to us to document and publish these events, we hold back, even in our own personal blog posts, even when the situation has been serious enough for us to switch companies or potentially derail our careers. Why do we do this?

The reason is simple: the tech industry is a lonely place for women to start with, and it gets immediately lonelier when facing harassment. Male and even female colleagues often dismiss you, saying, "He didn't mean it" or "You're reading too much into it," or even worse, "Can't you take a joke?" All these comments have one underlying theme: they make you feel like you are the one creating the problem. Meanwhile women are still working so hard to belong, to be part of the team, to "not upset the apple cart." And when they do report these crimes, too often the accuser gets more grief from the complaint than the accused, with formal and informal penalties ranging from demotions to being blacklisted as "difficult to work with."

Women will come forth to report harassment only when they feel safe to do so. That means working together, reaching out to other women, making our voices louder and clearer and our journeys less lonely. The more readily we report harassment with careful, detailed documentation of our claims, the easier it is for others to come forward. And as for those companies that penalize women who report harassment, they belong in court.

It surely won't come as a surprise that I frequently experienced innuendo, particularly in my early years in the workplace. At the time it seemed there never was any question that it was a burden I had to deal with alone, and so guess what? I became an expert at repelling advances. Given the egregious lack of support many women experience using formal channels to deter harassment, it seems worth passing on that wisdom as a tool to retake control in that moment.

A typical incident might look like this: a man who didn't know me well would approach me at a conference and say something like, "Wow, you're looking spectacular in that dress. I love how it hugs your curves. What are you doing after the meeting?"

My first rule of thumb was always *never engage*. There's no better way to control the situation. The moment you engage emotionally, whether with interest or anger, it is easy to become overwhelmed, and you lose control. Staying formal and keeping my distance, ignoring the overtones, and keeping the communication on the topic at hand worked well for me. I decided early in my career never to mix work with sex or romance. In these days of "always on" professional life, this could be more challenging than it once was. But for me, having that very clear line made it much easier to deal with situations when someone else tried to cross over.

In my earliest days handling innuendos was easy. Because English was my fourth language, I only interpreted what was said literally and responded back very literally. Often my language skills did not allow me to pick up the subtle suggestions being thrown my way.

That made it easy to dismiss and ignore anything potentially inappropriate and move on. Later I understood very clearly when someone was making a pass, but I consciously chose not to engage him, either positively or negatively. I perfected the blank stare back with complete lack of expression and no verbal response.

Another way I used to throw cold water on an innuendo was to ask, "Can you please explain what you mean by that?" That enabled me to keep the conversation formal, detached, and out of the emotional realm. They got it. In fact, there's no faster way to get someone to switch the subject.

I came to develop a persona in these instances that probably most resembles a very gracious Spock, a neutral and detached observer from a distant planet. I'd say no, in clear, plain language with absolutely zero emotion. I wouldn't show discomfort or judgment; I'd just move the conversation elsewhere. And I never had a guy try twice.

I realized pretty quickly that most of the "bad" guys, those who purposefully cross the line with flirtation or other innuendo, aren't enemy robots, programmed for only one goal with women. They can be converted. Flirting is an enticing experiment, even a game: *What will happen? Will she go for it?* In other words, they measure their behavior according to yours. You can drive the interaction wherever you want it to go. This is not to say the behavior is harmless or acceptable—actually, it's egregious—only that it doesn't render you, the woman on the receiving end, powerless. Think of it as a dance where your moves are just as defining of the dance as his are.

If we operate from the point of view that we are in control, then we have no real enemy, only obstacles to be managed. Adopting that attitude, I frequently developed comfortable, respectful working

DON'T WAIT TO CORRECT BAD BEHAVIOR

Claudia Fan Munce, today a venture capitalist at New Enterprise Associates following more than thirty years at IBM, has had plenty of opportunities across her long, successful career to hone her response to inappropriate remarks. Her most important takeaway? Train yourself to react to the behavior in real time. If something makes you uncomfortable, don't overthink your response. It's way too easy to talk yourself out of saying anything. Instead, jump right in.

"Call attention to the behavior immediately," says Claudia. "Say something like, 'Wow, I hope you didn't mean to do that' or 'I don't appreciate this. I know you will respect that.'" Claudia has also had success using humor to allow the person to back out, saying something like, "Hey, this feels like harassment—are you looking to have an appointment with our head of HR?"

relationships with men who initially had other kinds of "collaboration" in mind.

If you experience sexual harassment—I'm hopeful that today this is an *if,* not a *when*—my personal advice is this: respond in the way that powers *you* back UP. This will be different for every woman. Retake control, whether that means a very firm yet polite "no," a visit to HR, or a visit to your lawyer. Do recognize that formal allegations, in which you document the harassment and report the individual, are more likely to lead to real change that protects not just you but other women in the organization as well. Not every woman will be willing to divert her attention and take on that risk, and we all have to choose our battles. Men, after all, have always had the privilege of focusing single-mindedly on their career, why shouldn't we?

But know this: we are all indebted to those women who do step up, often at great personal cost. Let's all work together to make the path less lonely.

4

How to Get an A in
Attitude and an F in Victim

Have you ever had to charge forward with a positive attitude when you have every single reason in the world to doubt yourself? Welcome to entrepreneurship, where staying powered UP requires you to recharge your own batteries. Again and again and again.

When we were raising investment capital for Salesforce, venture capitalists shut the door in our faces over and over. Today Salesforce is on track to becoming a $10 billion-plus revenue corporation, so when I tell people this, they have trouble wrapping their heads around it. But through a period of several years and dozens and dozens of meetings, we heard many different versions of no over and over again. No one believed corporations would ever allow their crown jewels—sensitive customer data—to be stored on servers owned and hosted by a third party, especially a no-name startup.

All those *nos* provided myriad opportunities for us to second-guess ourselves, to say, "If the guys who are in the business of making money think we can't make money, maybe we should listen." I had many, many sleepless nights and a lot of anxiety. I know Marc Benioff did as well, especially during a "bet the company" moment, such as when we transitioned the company from telesales to an enterprise direct-sales model. Ray Lane, a partner at the famed venture firm Kleiner Perkins, told us this was "corporate suicide." He was among many who counted our low-cost telesales model, with its short sales cycle, among our core competitive strengths.

Marc believed that if our goal was ultimately to serve not just small businesses but the large corporations of the world as well, we had to play the game like the big guys did, with an enterprise-quality field sales team. Hiring that level of sales talent would be expensive, and it would take time before that investment paid off. You don't sell enterprise packages in a phone call; it takes time to build a relationship and even more time for a big company get internal consensus around any new solution. Ultimately I was among the majority who backed Marc's vision to move to an enterprise sales model, which made us a high-revenue-growth company. Marc's willingness to fight for his vision—despite inevitable moments of doubt—is why Salesforce, not Siebel, is now the leader and giant.

It's a myth that entrepreneurs don't doubt themselves. Of course they do. I doubt myself all the time. I wake up in the middle of the night and can't sleep. I get paranoid. I hold myself to a very high standard and am constantly fearful I'm not meeting it. But I don't let it direct my action. I recognize it as the unfortunate but unavoidable side effect of being personally invested in a risky endeavor. When I wake up in the morning I charge forward as if the sleepless night never happened. I keep flowing, like the water my parents threw behind me when I was leaving for America.

So I kept moving forward with Salesforce. We all did. We focused on the work and found ways to do without venture or institutional money—which, by the way, we never got. We capitalized the company through individual investments, and then at the last round of private financing, a hedge firm came in when Salesforce's strategy was no longer seen as so risky.

Maintaining a positive attitude is hard for all entrepreneurs— and extra hard for women or anyone who views himself as an outsider or underdog. Underdogs are in a catch-22. Knocking down structural barriers and even unconscious bias against us requires an unflinching view into all the ways we're still held back. Yet advocacy and statistics have the downside of making us all hyperaware of the potential for myriad kinds of discrimination and sexism. It can feel incredibly defeating and deflating to our self-assurance. When we start to feel at the mercy of these forces that are outside of our control, we can feel like victims. We can become self-conscious and lose our confidence. We run the risk of stopping before giving it our all.

And so we wrestle with our attitudes. Venture capital investor Sonja Perkins tells women who want to make it in any kind of business to reset their expectations to "hard." Competing to win isn't easy and never will be. Says Sonja, "You have to get in the game.

You just have to do it. A lot of people are so worried, 'Is it perfect or is it not perfect,' or 'Am I going to get discriminated against or not get discriminated against?' Instead of worrying, just get in the game. Be like the pro football players. These guys know they'll get injured, but they get in the game and earn the rewards. By playing they have the chance to win."

A few weeks into Sonja Perkins's first venture capital job at TA Associates, she suddenly realized she was the only woman investment professional in the Boston office. She had a moment of crippling vertigo when she looked across the huge meeting table at the sea of men at her partners' meeting and thought, for the first time, *Was I hired to be the token woman?* Then she stopped and told herself to snap out of it. She gave herself a stern internal lecture: *I'm here, I'm qualified, and I'm going to believe in myself and win.* And she did.

Know the statistics, but do not let them stop you. Statistics are just numbers, they are averages, but they are not *you*. Be prepared to advocate for yourself and find ways to create your own frame of reference. How to maintain a positive frame when times—and people—are tough is the subject of this chapter.

BETTER A BITCH THAN A VICTIM

It's hard to maintain a positive frame of mind when dealing with the double standard that penalizes women for behavior that rewards men. There are times when we are forced to choose between being the bitch, the woman who righteously owns her power, and being the victim, who apologizes and smiles as her power is taken away.

Lara Druyan, a former technologist who now who runs the Royal Bank of Canada's Innovation Lab and Investments, can recall a key moment in her career when she had to decide *Am I willing to be the bitch?*

It was the late nineties, and Druyan was a product manager at Silicon Graphics, the Google of its day in terms of its reputation for cutting-edge innovation. Along with several other team members, she had been asked to speak to a group of about fifteen colleagues and managers one level up. That day she was the only woman presenting, and there was only one other woman in the room. One after another her peers spoke. The crowd was consistently quiet and respectful. When Druyan got up to speak she got a completely different reception.

"The room got noisy, people talking amongst themselves. When I started to speak it stayed that way," she said.

In an instant she had to decide how to react. As she saw it, there were two options, like a path in a decision tree: She could be "nice" and let it go, speaking to the few people who were still paying attention and hoping the others would eventually quiet. Or she could "be the bitch," as Lara put it, and ask the crowd to pay her the same respect shown to others before her.

So many women I know have found themselves caught in such moments. The "bitch" reputation tends to trail after women who are direct, assertive, go-getters; who stand up for themselves with confidence and daring; who compete fair and square; and who outshine their competition.

Many of these adjectives are what Stanford University's Clayman Institute for Gender Research refer to as *agentic traits*. The institute studies corporate performance reviews and found that women are often penalized for possessing these traits while men are rewarded and even promoted on the very same adjectives.

The word *bitch* itself is just the most crass expression of this double sexual standard that continues on, decade after decade, like a tenacious weed. In a professional setting you (hopefully) don't hear the dreaded "B" word much, at least not to your face. But high-achieving women nonetheless anticipate, fear, and face the negative consequences of the double standard. Women are expected to be communal in nature, expressed in attributes such as helpful, supportive, warm, compassionate, agreeable, friendly, collaborative, and so on. You get the picture. But Stanford's research shows that women are not promoted and cannot advance their career based on these communal traits, even though bosses like them—perhaps in part because they're nonthreatening. An interesting finding of the Stanford research is that the gender of the manager who is giving the review does not seem to make a difference in the way women are judged, suggesting both men and women share this bias.

A word about Lara, in case you're curious: she's the farthest thing from a bitch that you can imagine. I have worked with her on several occasions, and she was probably the most soulful and sweet person I ever dealt with while working in venture capital. But what most stands out about Lara in my mind are her strong ethics and unflinching commitment to her values. Many investors are somewhat fluid in their values, but Lara has a strong moral compass and the courage to call dishonest people out. She's pragmatic, funny, and honest.

On that day at the front of the room Lara weighed her options and made a choice. She raised her voice and called out the crowd on their behavior.

"Excuse me. I would appreciate it if you would extend to me the same courtesy you extended to the speakers who preceded me," she told the room. "You asked me to speak here, so I assume you have an interest in what I'm about to say."

The room went completely silent. She ignored some dirty looks and launched into her presentation. The experience was stressful, but she left it feeling like she had stood up for herself. The decision she made that day was a choice she committed to going forward: better a bitch than a victim.

"I'm a pretty nice person, so it's not like I relish it. But I'm willing to go there and embrace that if that's what I need to do to be heard, to make a point, to get something done," she says. Lara is not confused about when to be assertive to get the attention she deserves.

On some fundamental level we all want to be liked—loved, even. That's not female; it's *human*. Meanwhile to be a bitch is to be completely unlovable. That's what gives the word its teeth. But the more of us who make the choice to stand up and be heard, despite the consequences, the less any of us will need to fear it.

When the word fades into history we'll still have the challenge of keeping our confidence and sanity when a colleague plays dirty. That won't change, and it's not really a gendered problem; power games are a reality of competitive environments. However, they may affect women more profoundly. Studies have shown that the critical opinions of their peers influence women more than they do men. In one recent study of 221 MBA students, women and men were asked to rate their leadership skills as well as that of their peers. At the beginning of the experiment both men and women tended to rate themselves significantly higher than their peers did. But over time women downgraded their original self-assessment much more dramatically than men did.[1]

I'm a confident, secure person, probably thanks to a combination of inborn stubbornness and my father's adoration in childhood. And yet there have been many times when I've had to fight to keep my confidence in the face of criticism, delicious eff-you attitude or not. One time in particular stands out.

In my second job, at the startup, there was a woman—let's call her Jane—who saw me as her competitor. We had both gone to Stanford, and she seemed to feel like there was space at the company for me or her, but not both—an unfortunate effect of an earlier time when in some ways that was actually true. I was taking up some of the spotlight, and Jane felt threatened. She started telling everyone that I wasn't good enough technically to do my job and was making mistakes in my analysis of the operating system.

Suddenly people who had taken me seriously were now questioning my tech chops every time I pitched a solution or offered an opinion. And so for a few months I found myself constantly on the defensive, getting frustrated and irritable every time someone questioned me. I was expending a lot of energy being upset. Every time I defended myself I felt a little worse, and at some point I started wondering whether she was right: maybe I was lacking.

I finally stopped and took stock. I looked at the track record of my work and the feedback I had gotten from colleagues before this woman started her whispering campaign. My record told a much different story. At that point I realized that I had to stop being so defensive. Instead of setting my own agenda, I was wasting time fighting off the rumors. My distressed reaction was only validating the gossip.

With new self-awareness I made a conscious effort to take back the conversation. The next time someone questioned my ability, I didn't fight it. "I acknowledge your concern, but let's move forward and let my work tell the story," I said. Once I stopped talking about it, everyone else did too. Once I radiated the attitude, "This is not an issue," people started to believe me instead of her. And over time my work spoke louder than anything Jane could say.

It's not easy to brush off provocations. So many times it's the work itself that has saved me. When I start to get caught up in everyone else's opinions, I stop listening to the chatter and immerse myself in my work. Making progress restores my confidence and my belief in my own capability.

IN THE ROOM WITH INVESTORS

This is an exciting moment for female founders seeking investment. Women with years of venture investing experience and great track records are founding a new generation of venture capital funds. There's Aspect Ventures, founded by Jennifer Fonstad, formerly of Draper Fisher Jurvitson, and Theresia Gouw, formerly of Accel; Cowboy Ventures, founded by Aileen Lee, formerly of Kleiner Perkins; Female Founders Fund; and several more. Some are simply women led; others are focused on investing in female founders or in companies that focus on improving women's lives. They are all signs of a shift that will hopefully help ensure that women founders get the same shot that men do.

At the same time, the entire male-dominated industry is becoming conscious of the need to evolve. Some of them are even taking action to attract female general partners for the first time. Sequioa Ventures, whose senior partner notoriously claimed they'd hire more women if only they could find some up to their standards, is among them.

As important as this shift is, I'm not sure it will make the confidence game of pitching any easier. It is always hard. You're meeting with people who could change your life—if they choose to. You have the dream, and they have the money, and thus, the power. Or so it seems. When that story mingles with repeated rejections, many potential founders give up quickly.

The founders who stay strong tell themselves a different story, one that gives them a lot more power in this balance. They prepare for meetings so that when they're in the room, they're cool, calm, and focused on what they have (the business that they passionately believe in), not what they don't have (the capital, market share, sales organizations, etc.). They hold onto this positive bent not just at their first pitch meeting, but at their thirtieth, after twenty-nine rejections.

The story these founders carry with them isn't David vs. Goliath or, for that matter, *Dana* vs. Goliath; they see themselves as being on equal footing with the people they're pitching. They're feisty and playing to win. Heidi Zak, for example, founder of ThirdLove, got familiar with rejection in early fundraising efforts for her software-enabled better-bra company. Meetings seemed to go well, but then a venture capitalist would say, "Hey, I don't think this is the right approach to the market," or "I don't believe your market sizing and technology are going to work," or "I don't think you can create better products than Victoria's Secret."

Here she was faced with smart, credible investors who had invested in plenty of start-ups and who, by passing, were telling her "Your business sucks." Rather than let them convince her, she took a stronger stance: "I had to want to prove them wrong." When she needed to stoke her confidence, she stopped worrying about the specific objections people had raised. Instead, she focused the conversation on the magnitude of the problem she was solving for women: finding a great-fitting bra without the need for an in-person fitting.

The strategy worked. As of August 2016 ThirdLove had received $13.6 million in funding from thirty-five investors, including a former Victoria's Secret CEO who apparently thinks ThirdLove can and will make a better product.

Lynn Jurich, the cofounder of the solar energy provider Sunrun, was even more deliberate in taking a competitive approach. "You always want to come in on the offense," she told me. When she pitched U.S. Bank for debt capital, no one was handing out money. The financial crisis had just leveled the world of banking. Meanwhile she needed $40 million to finance her customers' rooftop grids. She and her partner were the definition of desperate—this was their last and only chance at survival—and yet they walked into the room and made U.S. Bank's reps feel like they *might* have a shot at an incredible opportunity: "Here's the macro forces that we have at our back, here's why it makes sense, and here's why it's going to win over the long run."

Lynn didn't try to gloss over or avoid talking about the likely sticking points; instead, she and her partner prepared to hit those points hard. For example, they had to address the question of how the bank would get its money if Sunrun went out of business, given that their debt had twenty-year terms. And so they came with a list of several companies who could pick up the servicing if needed.

Feeling like you are worthy of competition becomes much easier the more you understand your "opponent." Lynn Perkins, the founder of UrbanSitter, told us that fundraising changed completely for her when she realized that venture capital firms weren't one size fits all. Different firms have different strategies and theses that guide their investments. In other words, getting turned down isn't really the equivalent of an investor saying, "You suck." It's more like dating: you're just not a match. Lynn started to see pitching as a puzzle: What was the investor's strategy, and how could she present Urban-Sitter in a way that would resonate?

INDEPENDENCE IS IMPOSSIBLE

Many entrepreneurs mistakenly think that as founders, they'll enjoy more freedom of independence. In fact, anyone building a company will find themselves to be more reliant than ever on the contributions and support of others. As the cofounder of Aspect Ventures, investor Jennifer Fonstad has watched dozens of early-stage companies find their footing. "Building a company has to be a group effort," she told me. "You need to pull in a lot of resources, call a lot of favors, and get humbled every day when people do not respond to your emails or return your calls. You need a lot of supporters, investors, advisers, mentors, early customers—those who believe in your vision and want to see it successful."

With experience Lynn also learned that not all venture capitalists were created equal. In the early days her attitude was "these guys walk on water." After several rounds of fundraising she understood that there are great venture capitalists and not so great venture capitalists. "I put a lot less pressure on myself," she told me.

Every fundraising founder gets better as she goes—and her product and business model often improve as well. Every investor will have a different take, but over time, if you're open to improvement, some feedback will resonate and stick. Heidi Zak told me that one of the first investors they met with criticized them for trying to launch with too many styles. At first she resisted the feedback. *Who would shop somewhere with only one option?* she asked herself. Over time she and her team realized that doing one thing well was in fact the best approach to make the most of their resources and to attract loyal customers. That became the launch model, and it has made for a better product.

No matter how well prepared you are, entering a room with people you don't know and asking them for money is frightening. Our animal bodies respond as though we're in mortal danger: our pulses shoot up and our hands get clammy, preparing us for fight or flight. However, science shows that stress can have benefits: a burst of energy, a sharp focus, and even a stronger immune system. The author and psychologist Kelly McGonigal has written an entire book on this, *The Upside of Stress*.

Leah Busque told me she stops her fear from paralyzing her by converting it to adrenaline. She told us about one of her most frightening moments as an entrepreneur. Early in the development of the idea that became TaskRabbit a friend had given her the email address of another friend, an entrepreneur she thought would like the idea. Leah wrote the guy a cold email, and they agreed to meet at his office, a hot young company called ZipCar.

It wasn't until the night before the meeting that she realized that he wasn't just an employee at ZipCar—he was the CEO, Scott Griffith. She couldn't sleep, suddenly afraid she was underprepared and would say something stupid in front of this person who was well positioned to help her with TaskRabbit.

That night she put into practice a routine that has since become second nature. "I'm not afraid—I'm excited," she told herself. "It's a really great opportunity, and I'm excited." In other words, she talks to herself about how excited she is until it's true. Fear becomes positive adrenalin. The next day she went into Scott's office, and they hit it off. Scott became a major supporter, even providing her a desk at ZipCar until TaskRabbit—which at the time Busque was calling RunMyErrand—had a space of its own. "Now, eight years later, I rarely feel that kind of fear or anxiety anymore. I trained myself to look at it differently," she says.

RIDING OUT BUSINESS LOWS

Even with a few successes under your belt, you'll always need strategies to recharge those batteries and keep your A for attitude. You're a lunatic until you're a genius, and sometimes even after you have been declared a genius you are sent back to being a lunatic. It takes courage to survive the initial lunatic years and even the later periods without burning out or giving up.

Earlier I mentioned that my own venture firm passed on Salesforce and that we managed to get by without venture funding. But there was one stretch when we almost *didn't* manage. When the dotcom market crashed in 2001 it took us to the verge of financial crisis.

> A daily self-care practice like exercise can turn things around when you feel like you're losing your personal grounding.

The trouble was that most of our customers *were* dot-coms, tech-savvy early adopters who were building their sales organizations, and now many of them were going out of business. At the time we were burning between $1 and $1.5 million each month, and with our customer base slowly dying off, we were cash-flow negative with no obvious sign of turning it around.

It was at this moment that I pitched the Salesforce.com opportunity to my partners, telling them that this would be a great time to invest, as the company was in need of cash and open to a new investment, which was an understatement. I vividly remember the horrified, skeptical looks on some faces as my colleague Jim Cavalleri, who was building the hardware to run Salesforce's software, presented our software-as-a-service (SaaS) model, with our customers' data stored in the cloud. They immediately asked us whether we'd be willing to license the software to large enterprises, letting them keep their customer and sales data behind their own firewalls.

Despite our financial desperation, the answer, both from Jim and me, was a loud and nonwavering *NO*. Software as a service was not just a buzzword or delivery model for us; it was our religion. We believed that the future of software development was nimble functionality, hosted and maintained by a technology company, creating dramatically better products and service. This vision was why I had invested.

After the Salesforce.com team left the presentation room my partners drilled me again, and I wouldn't budge. Finally one of them looked at me, exhausted, and said, "Are you not aware we've just been through a dot-com bust?"

I was deep in thought as I put my eleven- and thirteen-year-old boys to bed that night. I was sure we had done the right thing yet knew the tough cash condition the company was in. But unlike many other stressful nights when I lay with unproductive anxiety racing through my head, that night I just focused on the problem: *If investors wouldn't give us cash, where could we get it?* The answer I came up with led to a turning point in Salesforce's life.

We need to get creative and identify every single resource we have, I thought. That was when the light bulb went bright: though we were cash poor, we had a major asset: our customers. Those companies that survived the dot-com bust were delighted with our product and loyal because of it.

We had been offering customers a "pay as you go" payment model, something that had never before been done. It was a big attraction, as customers could quit completely or add or subtract users at any time. But as I thought about it I realized we could uncouple the cloud software offering from the payment model. I started thinking that we could move our customers from the pay-as-you-go model to annual or even multiyear contracts. We'd give them discounts for committing, and in exchange we'd get cash up front and continue to recognize the revenue monthly.

CELEBRATE THE SMALL WINS

It is nice to celebrate when you get a major win, like getting funding from an investor, doing a product launch, or getting a promotion. But those big wins are few and far between. If you wait for one to celebrate, you may be waiting a long time. So learn to set small goals that are achievable in a short period of time and celebrate each one.

I could hardly wait to put my thinking into a spreadsheet to model it out and see whether it would create a big enough cash infusion to save us from a potential bankruptcy. During the subsequent week I played with different customer conversion ratios to see their impact. My spreadsheet models proved that if customers signed discounted contracts and paid up front, we'd never need another penny of venture capital.

Elated by this discovery, I took my idea to Marc Benioff. I showed him that our monthly billing plan, intended to create a low-risk, no-commitment environment for our customers, was threatening the livelihood of our company. I believed we had proven our product's value to our customers sufficiently to have earned the right to ask for a contract and the upfront payment that came with it.

To say Marc was skeptical would be a major understatement. He had spent a lot of time and personal currency preaching the "no-contract, no-discount, one price for all" approach we had instituted. He thought changing it up could backfire. I argued that our cash crisis was real, whereas our customers' potential reaction was only a perception. Furthermore I pointed out that we would significantly reduce operational costs by moving customer billing from monthly to annual or even longer cycles. The more I spoke to Marc, the more committed I got to the new model I was advocating. And I truly believed that decoupling the hosted software and the no-contract billing would have no negative impact on our primary SaaS vision.

To Marc's credit, he was willing to consider the new strategy, despite the fact that he had deep and widely shared convictions around "no contracts, no discounts" and the new approach I was pitching cut against his deep conviction. We moved from consideration to execution very quickly when we found out that others, namely those in the sales organization, believed our customers would be open to signing multiyear contracts with upfront payments. As it turned out, they had been internally discussing the idea already as a way to stabilize the company's revenues. They had even gone as far as to analyze other companies who had similar approaches, and they shared these with us.

The rest, as they say, is history. With that one simple but significant change, Salesforce went from being deeply cash flow negative to cash flow positive in less than year.

Even though it's a moment I'm proud of—a fact I'm not afraid to share—my story isn't particularly rare. Talk to any founder and you'll hear hero tales, moments when only ingenuity and bravado saved a company from failure.

Lynn Jurich of Sunrun has one of those stories. Founded in 2009, Sunrun now operates the second-largest fleet of residential solar energy systems in the country and is growing rapidly. They have more than one hundred thousand customers across fifteen states; the only bigger provider is Elon Musk's SolarCity. And yet the road there has been incredibly tumultuous.

Before Sunrun it cost $30,000 for a homeowner to install a solar energy system on their rooftop, and once you had the system, you had to worry about maintaining it. Sunrun's innovation was to offer solar as a service. They install and maintain the system for free, then the homeowner pays for the electricity the system produces, at costs that are competitive or less expensive than the local grid. The model has allowed people who could never have afforded the cost or headache of solar to jump on board.

And yet when Lynn and her cofounder were just getting started and looking for input and investment, people were skeptical. Lynn called the entire Stanford alumni database for support as well as everybody else in utilities and energy.

"One hundred percent of people said it wouldn't work," she told me. "It wouldn't work, it wouldn't scale, we wouldn't be able to accomplish it."

Lynn's reaction? "Game on."

The pair plunged forward, convinced that the idea was good, regardless of whether industry incumbents could see it. They scraped together $3 million in angel funds, from their own pockets, and from people they'd worked with in venture capital. Lynn's former boss became one of the biggest investors.

The uphill climb only started there. Lynn and her colleagues have led the company through several crisis points since then. Even now, in a position of strength, Sunrun is weathering a plateauing market for solar but is doing it better than many of its competitors. How has Lynn continued to lead with the confidence, grace, and capability she's known for?

1. Listen to your customers more than your investors.

Industry insiders questioned whether customers would want Sunrun as a service. So Lynn went straight to the customer, setting up shop at county fairs and farmer's markets to sign people up. She got to know her customer intimately, and every interaction—and sale— helped her define the market's need. Handshake by handshake, she became more and more convinced that the venture was not just viable—it was the future of energy.

Soon she and her partner, Ed Fenster, had secured $12 million in financing, but to prime the pump, Sunrun needed more—just as the financial markets crashed in 2008–2009. Their business model required substantial debt capital. The company invests $30,000 for every rooftop system, and the money flows back in over twenty years of electricity payments. They need banks to make a bet that they'll be able to repay those loans.

Lynn's deep knowledge of her market and the customers she served paid off. As we saw earlier, she convinced U.S. Bank, one of few institutions that wasn't exposed to subprime mortgages, that there was a growing market for their service and that their customers could be trusted to pay their electricity bills. Not only did Sunrun get the backing they needed—a $40 million round—the doors of every banking institution slammed behind them, shutting competitors out.

2. Ground yourself with exercise, meditation, and self-care.

Once the company got its footing, it grew rapidly, with the exception of one year. That one year was a tough one for Lynn. She was struggling with a personal issue unrelated to the business and at the same time needed to keep employees and investors confident during this patch of low growth. Some of her executives were "very, very unhappy" with her, questioning her ability to lead. "It was just one of those times when you feel that everything is crumbling in on you," says Lynn.

For the first time ever she was failing to manage the confidence game. Her anxiety was taking on a life of its own. She committed to finding a solution, and she did. Lynn turned to meditation or, as she puts it, "mind control." She's a competitive, achievement-oriented person, so dedicating time to the pursuit of equanimity, balance, or some other woo-woo notion was always going to be a hard sell. She wouldn't sustain it. But mind control? This was like a CEO superpower, with clear and immediate benefit. Mind control she could devote herself to. She read several books, hired a yoga instructor, and carved out the time. Now, several years and her first child later, she says meditation got her through that difficult year, and she's still a committed practitioner.

Whether it's meditation, yoga, or exercise, a daily self-care practice can turn things around when you feel like you're losing your personal grounding. Personally, I like to hike in nature. "It's about taking time to separate your thoughts from who you are," says Lynn. Her recommended starter text is *Open Heart, Open Mind* by the Tibetan Buddhist Tsoknyi Rinpoche.

3. Let the vision renew you.

In 2015 Sunrun entered the public markets, introducing the company to new sources of volatility. Even though the company's share value fell (along with that of every public solar provider), Lynn was able to keep investors, employees, and herself confident by focusing on the company's mission: to create a planet run by the sun. In a startup landscape where so many CEOs are focused on "the exit," Lynn is building for the future.

"Things don't shift quickly. We're actually switching faster to distributed local clean energy than I thought we would," she says. "But it's a decades-long mission. I spend a lot of my time and energy focusing on maintaining the equanimity of the long-term vision for the company. That can be hard. That can be hard when you're living quarter to quarter and when the market is challenging. But we make the right moves now to build the value a decade out."

Gina Bianchini, the cofounder of Ning, and more recently, Mighty Networks, expressed something similar when she told me that confidence isn't an "input" but an output—the result of having a vision and a passion that light you up. In her case that passion is helping people connect. "The input for me is I want to live in a world where people can instantly meet each other around a shared interest or a shared identity," she says. "I have been working on this specific problem, challenge, opportunity for twelve years. I plan on working on it in some way, shape, or form for another twelve years because I think it is so important."

When confidence wanes, remind yourself *why* you're doing what you're doing—and press forward. Purpose is among our most potent ways to power UP. It radiates like light, drowning out any dark thoughts that might render us victims, not victors. Purpose also lights up the room, drawing others to your side exactly when you need them most.

5

People Power

If you want your career to take off quickly, you need people power: a close inner circle of individuals who want to see you power UP almost as much as you do. Think of them as your flight crew, a handful of helpers who know exactly what's needed for liftoff—and take action to make it happen.

First, though, it's important to understand what people power *isn't:* it is *not* an excuse to put the responsibility for your success in the hands of anyone but yourself.

Most recent career books and professional development programs will tell you that the most important person on this crew is a great mentor. Not only is that false, but I've seen it lead to strange behavior and a troubling mindset. I didn't have anyone who came close to fitting the traditional description of *mentor*, an older professional formally taking a young person under their wing to offer advice and coaching. Many of the women I interviewed said they never had a formal mentor either.

Meaningful mentorship requires a commitment of time and care. It's a fairly intimate relationship, which is why many women I spoke to said that many friends and trusted coworkers provided the kind of guidance we associate with mentorship. Yet the pressure to find that mythical beast, the Mentor, has led many otherwise socially well-adapted young people to write cold emails to near strangers asking them to fulfill this role. I've received several such requests. It's an awkward exchange for both parties.

In corporations, formal mentoring programs for women haven't leveled the gender playing field. These programs were intended to give women support and visibility to rise into senior leadership positions. And yet a 2010 survey by the women's advocacy group Catalyst followed men and women in a high-level mentoring program at a large multinational.[1] After two years in the program the men had received 15 percent more promotions than the women. Meanwhile many women feel like they're being "mentored to death," according to a recent HBR article, wasting time on meetings and commitments that didn't ultimately advance their careers.[2] Patronizing coaching prep work is eating up time that could be spent strategizing or getting good work done.

What's more, overemphasizing the "magic bullet" of mentoring can lead you to take on a passive mindset. People start to look at a mentor as a kind of fairy godmother who solves every problem and opens every closed door. Gina Bianchini of Mighty Networks told me she has met young people who seemed to be looking for a parent at work, "someone who'll take care of everything for you in the same way that your parents used to take care of everything for you in your younger years."

So stop yearning for mentors, those benevolent souls who advise you over tea and crumpets. First, focus your ambition on generating good ideas and developing your skills and experience, and with that, your self-belief, awareness, and intuition. Learn through action, and become your own wise guide. Those who take ownership of their careers open their own doors. They discover that powerful relationships are an *effect* of their progress, not a prerequisite for it.

With this mindset you are perfectly positioned to build people power. Undeniably there are moments as you build a career or a business when the support of powerful people can quickly launch you forward. But these people aren't mentors; they are *sponsors*. This relationship is often conflated or confused with mentorship because great mentors often serve as sponsors too. But the contribution of a sponsor is very specific. These are the people who don't just help you with advice; they actively advocate for you, using their position to secure opportunities, promotions, and introductions. Sponsorship, it turns out, is among the reasons men rose higher than women in that Catalyst study—they were more likely than women to be sponsored. Understanding the difference is incredibly important because it affects how you choose, nurture, and measure the success of your professional relationships.

YOUR FIRST SPONSOR IS YOUR BOSS

In *Lean In* Sheryl Sandberg writes about the importance of giving back. When she describes mentoring a handful of bright young people, it's quickly clear that she's done much more for them than that. She got one a job at Facebook, introduced another to his current venture capital partners, and put another on the short list to join the board of Starbucks. She sponsored these individuals, using her social capital and professional reach to create concrete opportunities. That's a much more bold, generous use of her influence than lending advice or even friendship, even though I know her sponsors deeply value those gifts as well.

Notice that two out of the three mentees Sandberg mentions are former employees. That's no accident. "Sponsor" sounds formal and removed—a daunting relationship to develop. So put it aside and instead focus first on finding a really great boss. After all, you don't get sponsors, especially ones as powerful and committed as Sheryl Sandberg, by writing emails or completing professional development worksheets. You get them by earning their belief that you'll represent them well in the world. There's no better way to do that than by doing great work for them.

Really perform for someone, and they'll go out of their way to make sure the work is beneficial for you too. Lara Druyan told me that early in her career she had a great experience at a company despite the fact that it wasn't a great cultural fit. She had had some uncomfortable run-ins with a middle manager who played power games by teasing personal information out of young analysts and using it against them. Lara refused to engage with him, and he didn't like it. He could have made her job difficult if it weren't for the protection of the leader Lara did most of her projects for. "I did great work for him, and through that work I got to know him personally," she says. "He protected me from that middle manager and wrote my business school references." In fact, decades later he still serves as a reference.

So if you're working in an organization, don't make the mistake of thinking that your best sponsor is somewhere far removed from you. It's probably either your boss or, even better, a more highly placed senior leader who you work with directly. It's true that the more highly placed your sponsor, the more doors he or she can open.

> The most lasting professional relationships grow out of truly great work.

But the quality and depth of the relationship will determine the degree to which they put themselves on the line for you. That's why I've said that you'll get the highest impact from finding a great boss or tapping the relationships you already have.

Bosses are the people who know your work well enough to be able to confidently recommend you for challenging projects and positions. And if you've contributed to their success, they're likely to care and want to help when you share your own professional goals, even if those goals will eventually lead you away from the company. Certainly there are bosses who don't reciprocate in this way. They're bad bosses, and I truly believe that one of the best career moves you can make is to find a good one. If your boss isn't sponsoring you, it's also possible you haven't yet earned the right to ask for his or her sponsorship.

So how do you earn it? What does it mean to contribute to your boss's success? Doing a great job is only the baseline. You need to find ways to make their job easier. Do jobs no one else wants to do. Solve problems you weren't asked to solve but clearly contribute to business goals and specifically, to your *boss's* goals. Earn their respect and their allegiance.

Career books often tell you to build a better relationship with your boss by getting personal—asking them to coffee and remembering their birthdays and their children's names. Although those human connections are nice and make work more pleasant, the most lasting professional relationships grow out of truly great work. If you can help move your boss forward professionally and contribute significantly to your company or your department's success, you're contributing more to his or her personal life than you do by exchanging personal chitchat.

SEEK HYPER-LOCAL SPONSORSHIP

By definition, entrepreneurs don't have a "boss," particularly in the founding stages of their business. That presents a special challenge in finding great sponsors. And yet for anyone launching a business, sponsorship is incredibly important. Social capital drives the world of venture capital. Venture capitalists get thousands of pitch emails sent their way. The handful they take seriously—the ones they actually read and respond to—are almost always the ones who come in from another investor or entrepreneur whom they take seriously.

The support of a powerful sponsor also goes a long way especially when self-doubt bubbles up and you're asking yourself, *Am I crazy?* Michelle Zatlyn, the cofounder of Cloudflare, told me that when she was teetering back and forth between pursuing her business and taking a job at LinkedIn, the sponsorship of a venture capital firm, Highland Capital, gave her the confidence to keep going. The opportunity to join their summer incubator program for students made turning down a great job actually seem legitimate.

So the question is, How do you get on the radar of sponsors who can take some of the friction out of your journey forward? We know generic emails don't work. The key, I've found, is what you might call hyper-local targeting: forging relationships with people who are so closely linked to what you're up to that you already share interests and even operating principles. These are the people for whom your work and knowledge are uniquely valuable and vice versa.

Hyper-local interest is how I ended up in business with Dan Lynch, the relationship that was probably most influential to my later success as an entrepreneur and investor. I met Dan through his son, whom I had worked with on a consulting project when I owned my own consulting firm. He told me that his father had just sold InterOp, his tech trade show, and was toying with a new networking concept. He was looking for someone like me, an operationally driven technologist, to collaborate and exchange ideas with. At the time I did not have employees, and my consulting project was coming to a close, so I was open to trying something new.

Dan knew everybody in the Valley. He was also a lot of fun and a very creative thinker. We both felt we would get along well and complement each other. It was immediately clear to me that working with him would be a blast and that he could add a lot of value to my career. His reach was much larger than mine. Here was my chance to leap back into the world of technology startups, having received my "free MBA" as a consultant, first working for Booz Allen and then running Management Forum, my own firm.

Meanwhile Dan saw that I could be the great execution partner he needed to make things happen. Dan had many great ideas but trouble executing them. He dropped a lot of balls, and he realized that I would not hesitate to catch them and run them forward. Later, when we started working together, he'd tell people, "I make the promises. Magdalena keeps them." And it was true: he'd promise a lot of things to a lot of people, then I'd have to deliver.

Pursuing people hyper-local to your own business interests strengthens sponsor relationships in a few ways.

YOUR KNOWLEDGE IS UNIQUELY VALUABLE. I offered more than sweat equity. I had been very conscious about staying visible in the world of technology and carving out a specific niche where I could confidently claim expert status despite the fact that I had taken time off after my second child's birth. Visibility is incredibly important not just for entrepreneurs but for intrapreneurs too. That means not just doing good work but also doing work that earns you public recognition in the circles that matter to you.

A year before I met Dan I had embarked on an independent research project to build my personal brand recognition. I was self-employed at the time, earning money as a consultant. I created and deployed a user survey to gather data about who exactly was using the Internet and how. It was the first-ever Internet user research of any kind, and what I learned uniquely positioned me to help create one of the world's first commercial Internet providers. Dan knew of my work and the respect I had garnered in his industry because of it. When we started talking together about creating the very first for-profit Internet access provider, I was able to assure him that the number of Internet users was growing quickly enough that the law restricting commercial use would soon be overturned. I had seen it in my research.

So Dan proposed we partner to start a revolutionary new company together, one that would offer Internet access to businesses for the very first time. He would have 90 percent of the company we were founding together, and I would have 10 percent. Even though the partnership was far from equal, I was so thrilled with the opportunity that I didn't even think about negotiating the split. And even though Dan had just made tens of millions of dollars selling his company InterOp and I barely had a savings account, I didn't balk at not being paid either. After all, we were cofounders, both of us taking a risk, and we leaned heavily on Dan's substantial social capital and reputation as we met with Internet access providers at universities such as Stanford and MIT. I felt great about the partnership and was grateful to work with such an industry leader on an opportunity I believed would change the world.

SERENDIPITY REPLACES STALKING. When your interests are closely aligned with your potential sponsor, those interests will bring you together seemingly magically as long as you're out in the world actively pursuing your goals. You won't need to stalk them, by which I mean digging until you find their email or phone number and then sending a cold intro. If you network enough, others will push you toward them. You don't even need to be well connected. That was the case for Leah Busque, the TaskRabbit founder, when she met Scott Griffith of ZipCar. At the time she was so passionate about her business idea that she was talking to "anyone who would listen," including the mom next to her in the coffee shop or the guy on the bus. She didn't have many entrepreneurs in her network, and she certainly didn't know any venture people.

Leah's husband, however, worked at a healthcare startup. As I wrote earlier, one of his colleagues gave her the email of the CEO of ZipCar. There was a very specific reason why she correctly guessed that he would be excited about Leah's idea. TaskRabbit was an online network to facilitate local connections. ZipCar's network of cars similarly relied on hyper-local geography. Although the businesses were very different and not competitive, they were both animated by ideas that were, at the time, pretty novel. Ruzwana Bashir, the founder and CEO of Peek.com, a one-stop shop to book activities and experiences, is a Brit of Pakistani heritage who now lives in California. She told me that she often receives cold emails from women who say, "I am so much like you—I am also Pakistani," or "I am also British and moved to America." Because of this overlap, they want her to mentor them. "They don't come with a specific request that I am uniquely able to help them with nor an approach that suggests that it could be a symbiotic relationship—it feels like it's all 'take' rather than both parties giving," she says. She is warmed by their interest, but she doesn't have enough hours in the day to devote herself to mentoring strangers rather than the eighty people in her team at Peek. She rightly points out that ethnic or national overlap has little to do with mentoring someone professionally. What matters is sharing common professional objectives, not common heritage.

YOU DON'T HAVE TO WORK AT RAPPORT. Many books offer networking advice about how to create instant rapport by sharing personal details or asking the right questions. Although I'm sure the advice can be helpful, what I find is that rapport comes naturally and often immediately when your professional interest uniquely overlaps. You're better off finding those people in the crowd than looking for ways to become buddies with any VIP you can get your hands on.

Conferences are good places to find people with whom you share interests. But being in the presence of high-ranking people doesn't get you much. To establish quick rapport you also need credibility. For instance, that Internet study I conducted got me a presentation slot at the very first Internet conference in Washington, DC, and being a presenter gave me validity with the other attendees. It put me in a completely different position as I networked my way through the event.

Clara Shih is among those whom Sheryl Sandberg mentions mentoring in *Lean In*. They first met at Google, Clara's first job out of college. But they didn't have a relationship until several years later when Clara bumped into Sheryl at a conference. They no longer worked for the same company, but in some ways they now had more in common. Sheryl had just started working at Facebook; Clara was deep into her first book, *The Facebook Era*. With professional interests so closely linked, they immediately had a lot to talk about. A relationship unrolled naturally from there. When Clara was deciding to leave Salesforce to start a social media consultancy, Sandberg wasn't just encouraging (like a great mentor); she introduced Clara to her first investor (like a great sponsor).

When it comes to building sponsor relationships, "There's got to be some baseline level of chemistry," Clara told me. "You can't force it. Sometimes you just have that chemistry with someone, and sometimes you don't." Although that's certainly true, I've found that intersecting professional interests create the best chemistry. They also ensure that your potential sponsor has relationships that actually matter to your business.

NO MENTOR? NO PROBLEM. As your business matures, you may find that your best sponsors—the ones who are willing to mentor you as well—are those who have stepped up to put real skin in the game. It makes the two-way nature of the relationship formal, which for many people is a big comfort. Ruzwana, for example, told me that she did not have mentors early in her career. In fact, she thought she might never have one.

Like me, Ruzwana is accustomed to being an outsider. She grew up in the very closed Pakistani community in England, wearing the hijab every day and attending mosque after school. Her father, who supported the family selling vegetables in the local market, and her homemaker mother saw their smart daughter receive the best marks both in her public school and her mosque school. Ruzwana's high school honors led to university at Oxford. At Oxford she started wearing Western clothes and enjoyed the wonderful freedoms of the intellectually progressive community. But there were still times when she was made to feel like an outsider—most notably when she ran for president of the Oxford Union and her opposition tried to undermine her by publishing in the student paper an old picture of her in a hijab, implying that she was not one of "them" and therefore unfit to lead. She won anyway.

Keeping her own frame of reference in such moments gave Ruzwana an uncommonly strong bent of self-reliance. "I did everything for myself and didn't expect anything from anybody else," she told me about that period of her life. Even now she's careful to not expect others to provide a lot of help.

Nevertheless, not having a mentor didn't hold her back: she went from Oxford to Goldman Sachs and Blackstone, then to Harvard Business School, and finally the world of startups. In recent years she's been celebrated in *Fortune, Vanity Fair*, and *Fast Company* as one of the Valley's hottest young entrepreneurs. And now, for the first time in her life, she has a sponsor who is also like a mentor she can call on. He's an investor and board member at Peek. He's not her first investor, but he is the first who has shown he has the time and energy to be proactive, listen, and offer day-to-day guidance. She feels comfortable going to him for advice because he's literally invested in her success—if she wins, he wins.

THE PLACE FOR MENTORS

I did eventually find a sponsor who also was a mentor, as I mentioned, so I can say with confidence that having the ear of a wise and caring professional elder is a wonderful thing. Irwin Federman was a senior partner at U.S. Venture Partners. We met because USVP had been interested in investing in MarketPay, the company I launched after CyberCash. When I ended up selling it before I had even finished the prototype, USVP switched gears and asked me to join the firm. Irwin was the one who talked me into it. I really think I took the job only to have the chance to learn from him. I would have carried the guy's bags if it meant a few more minutes to listen. He is a philosopher as much as a venture capitalist, with a unique perspective that always soothed whatever my worry was that day. I took to jotting down the things he would say in a notebook, which I labeled "Irwin's Pearls of Wisdom." *When in doubt, do without* was a favorite maxim, along with *You get nothing for just trying.*

I was cautious not to impose on his time and was highly attuned to the value of each minute I had with him. No topic was off limits in our conversations, which gave me insight to his thinking on more than just the nuts and bolts of business dealings. He shared even his most painful personal experiences with me so I could learn from them. I still do today. When the two of us have lunch I always walk away having learned something, wishing I had more time with him but grateful for each impactful moment.

When you are lucky enough to meet such a person the last thing you want to do is scare them away by asking them to conform to some kind of formal, structured mentoring program. Wise people are rare, and the time you have with them can be transcendent. You don't "pencil them in"; you find ways to join their mission so a relationship can grow naturally.

The best mentoring relationships might be better described as true friendships. Heidi Zak of ThirdLove told me that she has always found the word *mentor* "a little bit strange." It sounds formal and static, whereas her experience has been fluid, with numerous friends, peers, and colleagues stepping into the role of trusted adviser in the moments when she needed one. That said, she has had one relationship that could be described as mentoring: Lisa, her first boss. But today Heidi thinks of Lisa first and foremost as a friend.

Heidi started her career after college as an analyst at an investment bank. She reported to Lisa, an associate straight out of business school. Heidi immediately looked up to Lisa, an incredibly hard worker who was successfully building her career while having kids. When it came time for Heidi to plot her next move, the first person she went to for advice was Lisa, who encouraged her.

Over the years Heidi kept going back to Lisa when she faced one of life's big decisions. When she was deciding whether to leave a great position at Google to launch ThirdLove, she called Lisa, who told her to go for it. Then when she was deciding whether to have her first child during the first years of her business, she called Lisa, who again told her to go for it. "She told me, 'It's not going to be easy, and it's not going to be pretty. You'll make sacrifices on both sides, but you can do it.' Her advice was not to wait until the timing was right to have kids, because the timing would never be right. This was in my mid-thirties."

Heidi says she has always thought of Lisa as a friend. But these days the relationship feels on more even footing than ever. She's finally finding herself in the position of experienced-advice giver instead of recipient. First she helped Lisa with advice about the equity offer she had received from a startup looking to hire her. More recently she wrote a recommendation letter to the dean of the business school where Lisa is now a finance professor.

"It's really great to be able to help her continue her path and for her to continue to help me. That's a friendship, right? She's a friend, and I love her," says Heidi.

The best mentorship isn't an "ask"; it's a friendship, fluid and voluntary, based on mutual goals and convictions. When you find such a friend, celebrate—and be open and free with your gratitude.

THE POWER OF OTHER WOMEN

There will be inflection points in your career when you'll want to turn to women for counsel. Women-based communities are vital to helping us unpack some of the unique challenges we face. And just as you need to make an effort with men, here too you need to devote time and attention to building trusting, supportive relationships. Do not assume that just because someone is of the same gender as you that they are going to go the extra mile to help you or advocate for you.

So many women told me about moments in their careers when another woman has played a special role in helping them move forward. Julia Hartz told me about the day an admired mentor grabbed her by the shoulders at a local café and convinced her that, yes, she was ready to be EventBrite's CEO. Heidi Zak told me she had fellow founder-mom Michelle Zatlyn's number ready to text at any time for advice—like the time she asked whether she should sit out a conference that would require travel two months after the birth of her second baby. (The answer: stay home.)

And perhaps most powerfully there was Sonja Perkins, who went through treatment for breast cancer in 2008, when her daughter was an infant. For the first time in her storied career in venture capital she realized the downside of not having a close female network. "I was not into women's groups," she says. "But I was lacking trusted close female friends who were professionals. I used to think, *Wouldn't it be great if I could just call Sheryl Sandberg? I bet she'd have some good advice for me.* I had few professional girlfriends—only a handful—to talk to. So I decided to change that and started Broadway Angels.

Sonja approached Jennifer Fonstad and me about joining her to start an angel group of investors and executives who happen to be women. All three of us had been general partners at Silicon Valley venture funds. In the years since, our members have invested in dozens of great companies, helmed by both men and women. (Lynn Perkins's UrbanSitter and Julie Wainwright's TheRealReal.com are both Broadway Angels companies.) Stanford Business School has written a case about Broadway Angels, and it has become one of the most popular that they teach. Harvard Business School teaches it too.

Broadway Angels has formal meetings to hear companies pitch, but much of the practical and emotional connection happens between meetings. As Sonja says, "We trust each other. It's all about business, but there are many other benefits that come from membership. I'm just so grateful for the many female friends and colleagues I have now who I did not have in those years of being a general partner in a venture fund."

So attend the many great conferences, events, and groups that have been organized to help women support other women. Have an ironclad circle you can trust to push you, cheer you on, and pick you up when you're down. Lean on women role models for inspiration and support. And as you make those connections, never miss an opportunity to pull a talented woman up with you.

There's one caveat to this advice: make sure you're not so focused on gender-based networking that you ignore those relationships—with men or women—that connect you most directly to capital, leverage, and market intelligence. When it comes to sponsorship, gender

DON'T WAIT TO ASK TOUGH QUESTIONS

Interviewing for a job is a two-way process: while the employer is assessing your capabilities and fit, you are assessing not just the company's overall culture but also your future boss and team members. It is your responsibility to ask specific questions that help reveal whether dysfunction and politics will be part of your everyday work life, covering topics like

▌ **POLITICS.** Who are the most influential decision makers? Which functions have the most pull? How does your team engage with others in the organization?

▌ **PROMOTIONS.** Is there a formal system for assessing performance, and if not, who and what drives advancement?

▌ **CULTURE.** What values drive decision making and working relationships? How have top people in the organization modeled those behaviors?

Don't be afraid of digging in, especially in startups, where there is infinite work and few employees or dollars to do it—an environment that often requires round-the-clock devotion. That kind of work-life imbalance is not for everyone.

could be considered a generic connection, not hyper-local at all. And yet most women I know who've had any public exposure around their success have been frequently approached by women exclusively on the basis of a gender connection. An older woman may be willing to make time to learn about a young woman's ambitions and goals, but unless she has highly targeted, relevant experience, the help she can provide is very limited. The ultimate return on the time invested does not go beyond getting a sympathetic ally or a "feel good" exchange. These relationships can be very enjoyable, but they often don't make any impact beyond that.

There's a bigger problem in exclusively targeting women as sponsors: you may be limiting your advancement. In that Catalyst study I referenced earlier, more women than men sought out women mentors—35 percent compared to 9 percent of the men. Meanwhile the most senior people in their companies were mostly men. This meant that overall the women had mentors who were less well placed to win them promotions. In other words, their choices might have been great as mentors, but they were less useful as sponsors. And sponsorship is what rockets you upward in an organization.

Perusing male sponsors is just as important if not more important for women entrepreneurs. Women may seem to be comfortable allies, but if you focus all your sponsorship efforts on the less-represented gender, you're at a major disadvantage. "If you just look at the data, there's just more men in positions of power," Gina Bianchini correctly points out. "It's a bigger market. There's more capital. And a lot of the women who have gotten into equivalent positions of power still have less capital."

Gina's point is all the more credible because, sponsorship aside, she recognizes more than most that there is special value in women helping women. Having founded two companies specializing in interest-based social networks, she put her professional expertise to work in support of women by cofounding Leanin.org with Sheryl Sandberg. At the center of that organization's mission, one Gina believes deeply in, is helping women find peers to support each other through gender-specific challenges. Countless women have been beneficiaries of Gina's work by connecting with each other.

Women absolutely play a unique and important role in helping each other. Just don't mistake it for sponsorship. Trust the men in your industry, develop friendships, enjoy their thoughts and companionship, and know that some will trust you back. It will feel good to network with men whom you may have thought were untouchable. Challenge yourself and reach out to one in your life. You have nothing to lose but a bit of time.

BUILD MOMENTUM
WITH THE RIGHT TEAM

Companies these days are looking for "culture fit" when they evaluate employees. You should too. A company culture in which you feel comfortable to be yourself makes powering UP so much easier. It's likely to be far more important to your forward momentum than any single mentor or sponsor.

When I started my career I didn't think this way—no one did. But these days the best companies take an active role in shaping their community, and some of them do much better jobs than others in creating a positive, inclusive environment that supports every employee, especially minorities. (You can read more about the best ways companies are doing this in Chapter 9.)

The people around you influence your attitude. After all, human beings are not atomized. Yes, you can create a distinct frame of reference within a negative environment, and a single voice can change a culture. If that weren't the case, I couldn't have survived at AMD. Nevertheless, it would be disingenuous not to admit that the culture of a workplace has a profound impact on how you feel about yourself and the quality of your work. Considering culture and coworkers when you seek out opportunities is one lever you can pull to make maintaining an attitude a great deal easier. When some companies are doing a great job supporting women and other minorities, why not seek them out? If more of the best and brightest "vote" for these companies, the more other companies will follow suit, recognizing a supportive culture as key to attracting great people. Think of a supportive culture as a critical line item on your pro-con list. What *supportive* looks like will be individual to who you are and what you need.

Caroline Simard, research director at Stanford's Clayman Institute, had a few suggestions to help women evaluate potential employers:

■ **HOW MANY WOMEN ARE IN SENIOR LEADERSHIP ROLES?** Clayman says this is often an indicator of how far along a company is in its journey toward equal opportunity.

■ **DOES THE COMPANY INVEST IN PROMOTING PEOPLE FROM WITHIN?** Ask about the process and opportunities for advancement.

■ **WHAT'S THE MANAGER LIKE?** This is particularly important if you're considering working for a large corporation, whatever its reputation. Says Clayman, "The reality is, these companies are very big, so even if you have great work-life policies in place, you may find yourself working in a specific pocket of the company where the culture is especially negative toward women who are parents," for example.

■ **HOW DOES THE TEAM FUNCTION?** You can ask the manager about some of the norms by which the team works together. How do you ensure that a person's voice gets heard? How do people contribute their ideas?

▍ **HOW ARE THEIR WOMEN DOING?** If you can, speak to women who work there and ask about their experiences and attitudes.

To this list I'd add a tip that's by no means backed by research but that several women I interviewed mentioned: if your boss is male, try to find out who his partner or wife is. If she's someone who has a strong professional background, he's much more likely to listen to you as carefully and as seriously as he listens to men. (I would never suggest using that as a sole criterion, but it's good data to have.)

All this said, there will be times when the effort of swimming upstream at a company—for example, in a "bro" culture run amok—will be worth it because the work opportunity is so uniquely suited to your goals. Other times you'd be better off finding a place that's a better fit. Lara Druyan, for example, decided that the patri-archal investment banking culture of Merrill Lynch in the nineties was not worth the fight. She had been recruited by a woman who had left by the time Lara started, leaving her as the only woman at the associate or VP level. When a coworker made a snide comment to another guy about "playing tennis with the girls," she called him on it. "I guess you didn't take diversity training?" she said. He stared at her and responded, "I guess you believed all that bullshit we told you in recruiting." Later she broke ranks during a blizzard by daring to wear a pantsuit instead of the skirt and heels customary for women in those days, and a supervisor scolded her for it.

At that point she began considering her options. If investment banking was her dream career, she might have stayed to fight. But she had chosen the path only because it was what "people did" when they graduated from Harvard Business School. She called a trusted friend in private equity to talk about it. "You're not a leverage-a-company-to-the-hilt, cut-a-bunch-of-people-from-the-payroll, and create-a-debt-instrument kind of person. What are you doing there anyway?" he asked her.

With his guidance she concluded that venture capital was a much better match for her interests. She quit Merrill Lynch, left the NYC blizzards behind, and never looked back.

Cultural fit goes beyond whether the company encourages and supports strong women. That's baseline. Imagine the difference in your attitude between working in a company that treats its junior employees as expendable and one that has an explicit goal of offering a transformative career experience for every employee. (That company exists: it's called Rent the Runway, and its CEO, Jennifer Hyman, has designed a culture, process, and workflow to maximize every employees' learning.)

You have the power to change a hostile work culture—and if not to change it, then to get what you need from it and move on. Both paths require courage, a strong self-belief, and a refusal to ever be a victim. Your ultimate destination is a team that nurtures your individual potential *and* allows you to imagine and conquer challenges that, alone, would be far beyond your reach. A team that helps you power UP.

Entering the Men's Room

For now, men still dominate the culture of the new economy. They've got the numbers, and women need to leap these cultural barriers to claim more space of our own. As Shirley Chisholm, the first woman to run for president on a party ticket, once said, "If they don't give you a seat at the table, pull up a folding chair." This chapter is all about how to do that: how to power yourself UP to join conversations, spaces, and events that, intentionally or not, seem designed to shut you out.

Claiming your seat at the table starts with a close look at how you're spending your professional social time. If you're like many women, you may be networking too much with women and not enough with men. This isn't just a guess; it has been quantified:

women are three times more likely to have a network that is mostly female.[1] This puts women at an immediate disadvantage because, as we already discussed, most of the people with power—the people who give you jobs and money—are men.

There are a lot of reasons why women end up with female-heavy networks. Overt sexism is, in my mind, the least influential. Ironically, the industry of women's networking events, conferences, and mentoring programs that have sprung up in reaction to sexism and with the goal of promoting women can also hold women back if they spend too much time in that refuge. A young man recently told me a story about being out to lunch with a group of young coworkers. It was a Friday, and a round of beers had added to the celebratory mood. Suddenly one of the young women at the table said, "Hey, it's one o'clock—we're supposed to be at that women's networking event." So all the women got up and left. The young men who were left behind ordered another round of beers, looked at each other, and concluded that this was now the men's networking event. Without meaning to, the company had created a gender divide.

Nevertheless, my hunch, supported by conversations with women and men I know, is that the number-one reason women network more with women is very simple: It's easier. It's comfortable. It's, well, fun. If you've ever been to a party that at some point in the evening, naturally divided between the sexes, you've seen a microcosm of this at work.

If you're in the first decade of your career, you might not have experienced this yet. It might sound conservative or even crazy. Male-female networking happens more naturally when everyone is single, no one has children, and most social events at work happen in the relatively gender-neutral territory of bars. And if after-work socializing leads to romantic escapades, it might even be considered a plus. (I won't judge as long as it doesn't get messy.)

That's less the case as you get older. As people marry off and have kids, it starts to be easier to spend your time, both professional and social, with the same sex. You don't need to worry about lines being crossed, people gossiping, or concerned spouses. Shortly after Dan Lynch and I started talking about working together, Dan told me that his wife wanted me to come to dinner. It was clear that she needed to vet her husband's potential business partner—who was half his age and the opposite gender. She grilled me for several hours to assess my technical abilities, business acumen, and my specific goals in having a close partnership with Dan. Ultimately she was convinced that my planned venture with Dan was not a cover-up for an affair. If she hadn't been, my working relationship with Dan would no doubt have been jeopardized. I respected her for taking the initiative and being open about doing what she needed to feel comfortable with the situation.

■ ■ ■

ADDING TO THE divide that comes with age, many women who never felt "gendered" suddenly feel different when they become mothers. Pregnancy, breastfeeding, and in many cases, the challenges of shouldering primary parenthood give new moms a lot in common with other women.

Aside from these practical divisions, working in male-dominated spaces at any age can be alienating. Occasionally that's because of overt discrimination. More commonly women face *micro-aggressions*, a word that didn't even exist when I started my career. At that time micro-aggressions were the lingua franca, so it didn't occur to us to call them out. The most identifiable and certainly funniest example of micro-aggressions I've seen was in Cate Burlington's article on the *Toast*, "Things My Male Tech Colleagues Have Actually Said to Me, Annotated."[2] On Cate's list

▌ "See, that's the great thing about you, I know I can tell 'offensive' jokes around you and you won't care."

▌ "I had this female boss once, and I know I'm not supposed to say this, but I could totally tell when it was her time of the month."

▌ "You and my wife could mud-wrestle naked."

Even if you can avoid or ignore asinine comments, you might feel the alienation of being "other" simply because you're different. You may not share the same cultural references, hobbies, or attitudes—or maybe you actually do, but the men you work with have trouble understanding that.

Typically my generation tried to erase or at least neuter their gender, an exhausting and often lonely experience that long ago entered the territory of diminishing returns. So what's the solution if you can't actually be gender-blind in your relationships with men at work?

You identify where the friction in mixed-gender networking lies and find ways to outsmart it.

BECOME AN INSIDER

We don't have total control over how others see us. But we can control the degree to which we see *ourselves* as outsiders. It's not easy when you're one of a few women in your cohort. And yet we all need to get our A in attitude on this because, otherwise, feeling "other" holds us back. It puts us at less than our best. It can become a self-fulfilling prophesy, leading us to segregate ourselves, which then widens the divide.

I grew up in Turkey as a member of the very small Armenian minority. The term *Armenian* was often used as an insult and even a curse word. I knew I was a second-class citizen. Despite this, I had and still have a very deep love for Turkey and the Turkish people. My entire childhood was a lesson in how to be comfortable and confident while being an outsider. I learned not to let people's initial negative attitude toward me shape my attitude toward them and others like them. I distinctly remember having sand kicked in my face when I was six years old because I did not have a Turkish first name and did not go to a Turkish primary school. But that didn't stop me from developing playmates on the very same beach and later, with the very same kids. I learned not to allow those initial negative encounters to get in my way of making new friends. What *I* wanted out of life drove my behavior, even at that early age.

Many times while growing up I dealt with people making negative comments about my ethnicity or religion. Every time I had to do the mental arithmetic to decide whether it was worth responding. Usually I let things slide, without bitterness, preferring to play the long game and focus on my goals. I often won the doubters over with time and with my ability to ignore the negativity and find common ground. Once I was their ally, I could make a much deeper impact on their attitudes.

All this served me well later in college and in my career. Being in a gender minority in Silicon Valley was comparatively benign. Aside from having the experience to deal with the occasional acute conflict brought on by simply being a woman, I had also long ago learned how to put others at ease with my otherness. In fact, I was so good at it that when I was the only woman in the room, the men lifted the filters on their conversation that they usually imposed in mixed company. I used to say I would someday write a book called *Things Men Say When Women Are out of the Room*. Believe me: I heard it all. And that was exactly what I wanted. Instead of worrying about how I felt, all my focus went toward making sure the men I went to school with and worked with felt comfortable to invite me in and be themselves. I let them know they should be comfortable saying anything they would around male colleagues. When talk got raunchy or obnoxious, I withheld judgment but also was comfortable being honest about how such behavior made me feel. I believed that the best way to be equals was to have full understanding of each other's attitudes and feelings. Without that, people would be guessing at each other's real thoughts and motives when full transparency would lead to better results. So long as my colleagues were respectful when addressing me directly, I was happy and felt safe.

If this sounds passive to you, rest assured: I was no victim. This approach was an active strategy. I recognized early that being accepted as one of the team would be essential for moving my career forward with the same speed—or faster than—my male colleagues. You don't get the ball passed to you if you're not seen as wearing the team jersey. If I made them uncomfortable, they would find ways to congregate without me. I'd be shut out of the informal conversations that led to future deals, partnerships, and general intelligence. Moreover, if I asked the men I worked with to restrict their comments, I couldn't be confident I'd get unfiltered honesty about things that actually mattered. Whatever they were thinking, they were thinking it. I might as well hear it all, I reasoned, instead of worrying about what was being said behind closed doors. I never felt comfortable with the idea that people I worked with should be able to say something to another coworker but not to me. It seemed clear to me that it could a career roadblock if I let it.

I'm not necessarily recommending this "anything goes" approach to women today. For one thing, if I had taken a more confrontational tack, I might have made faster progress toward a better workplace for women who were less inured to chauvinist remarks than I was. We have every right—and the responsibility—to step up and ask the management, which is most often white men, to partner with us in making a workplace that's inclusive not just of women but also of minorities of any kind. The key is to find a way to make this demand that keeps us all on the same team rather than making us adversaries or watchdogs.

If my story represents one problematic extreme, the hypercharged, litigious workplace atmosphere today represents another. Political correctness can be a gag order that restricts what people say without necessarily changing what they think. It may make us feel better in the short term but will backfire in the long run. I believe we will achieve true gender parity in the workplace when both men and women are able to see the virtue of having the job go to the individual with the best talent, regardless of gender, sexual preference, skin color, or any other superficial differences. True equality comes from appreciating each other's value to the organization's success, not from just using sanitized vocabulary. I see signs all around that we are becoming self-conscious and hypersensitive about gender and gender issues to the point of distraction, if not outright destruction.

As an example, I was speaking recently to a young woman who told me her "knee-jerk reaction" these days was to feel marginalized by her male peers. For example, if a man on the team thanked her for coordinating something, she'd take umbrage: "I didn't co-ordinate it. I provided the leadership." She was starting to feel like she was getting an A in victim. She was listening to men having conversations in the office and feeling, for no particular reason, like it was for "men only." In fact, all she needed to do to be part of the conversation was to speak up. "I need to find a way to be positive again," she said, "because as soon as I say, 'We're together on this,' the answer from these guys isn't going to be, 'No, you're a woman.'"

The question is, How do you hold your coworkers accountable to language and behavior that exclude others without causing them to feel attacked? How do you establish mutual respect and trust? There's no easy or right answer, but as we get into the nitty-gritty details, some tactics fall out.

MAKE ALLIES IN YOUR OFFICE

It's not easy to call out a colleague for sexist remarks or behavior. It's even harder to have your words lead to a change in their behavior. No matter how calm or firm you are, you'll often be met with defensiveness if not outright offense. Very few men think of themselves as sexist. Not the guy who "innocently" asks the only two women in the office to organize the annual canned goods drive for the poor because "you're so good at that kind of thing." (This happened to a woman I interviewed.)

To start, one strategy I recommend: get a man to do it with you or in your place. Why not share the burden? Establishing alliances with men whom you trust can be powerful. It allows you to have a voice in spaces where you might not otherwise. (Yes, including the men's bathroom!) There are actually two parts to this approach.

The first step is to find yourself one or several office allies. These are male colleagues with whom you develop a strong personal friendship. It's not romantic or sexual. You can speak to this person with no filter and trust him to be honest with you and not use your words against you. He is a confidante and not someone who controls your compensation or advancement. Someone who is an equal, not a boss.

Some people develop this kind of relationship naturally among close colleagues. But if you're the kind of person who feels like you can be your "real" self only at home, creating this kind of relationship is going to require a more conscious challenge. Like any relationship, you'll need a period of courtship: small moments when you let down your guard and share honestly about the challenges you face, together and separately. Once you see whether these conversations are kept confidential and become more comfortable, you can extend the trust to a wider set of topics.

I would have had a much tougher time making it in venture capital without the partner who was my de facto work husband. Aside from being able to gripe to him about the double standards I faced as a mother, he also saved me from falling into "Magdalena bashing." When I was new to venture capital I developed a terrible, nonproductive practice of brutally criticizing myself and taking responsibility for my portfolio companies' problems. It was a self-destructive behavior that often led to me feeling highly disappointed in myself. With his help, I learned to avoid this useless negative behavior that wasted so much of my time and energy.

This level of relationship with the other gender will help not only to reduce sexist remarks in the workplace but also to deal with the "other" burden in general. Maybe you've heard of the Gallup organization studies that have shown that people who have a best friend at work are more productive, passionate, and loyal to their organizations. (Interestingly, the studies actually showed that "best" was a stronger predictor than "close "of all the mentioned benefits.) Additionally, people with a best friend at work are

▎ 43 percent more likely to report having received praise or recognition for their work in the last seven days;

▎ 37 percent more likely to report that someone at work encourages their development;

▎ 28 percent more likely to report that in the last six months someone at work has talked to them about their progress;

▎ 27 percent more likely to report that their opinions seem to count at work;

▎ 21 percent more likely to report that at work they have the opportunity to do what they do best every day.[3]

Gallup's engagement studies don't take gender into account. But I encourage women to choose a man as your "bestie" and confidante for a few reasons. First, with a close ally you're much less likely to feel like an outsider even if you're the only woman.

Consider the programmer who told me she had good work camaraderie with her team, which was all male. Nevertheless, things suddenly turned awkward every time her manager broke out a bottle of Scotch for after-hours team bonding. "I felt like I didn't belong," she told me, and she would often excuse herself, missing out on the chance to become closer with her colleagues and manager. If I had been her friend and mentor at the time, I would have urged her to get to know someone in the group well enough so she'd never feel outside the circle—even if Scotch wasn't her drink or she didn't drink at all.

Another great argument for cultivating a male best friend at work: you'll get a friendly window into another perspective—a spy in the locker room, so to speak. When you have established enough trust to be honest with him, you'll get the same in return. And as with any confidante, male or female, he might help you see patterns in your own behavior to self-correct.

TREAT YOUR ASSISTANT AS WELL AS YOUR BOSS

No matter their title or corporate position, everyone is a potential ally. I once fought to get executive assistants invited to a "professionals only" party. No one should be made to feel like they're outsiders, not fit for a company event. They worked as hard—some even harder—than the rest of us and deserved to be included. This did not lower my stature. Quite the contrary: it won me respect among the senior people who mattered. And it won me loyalty and true friendship among our administrative staff.

Finally, a work spouse is someone who you can easily activate as a gender ally. Here's someone with whom you can be honest about your experience as a woman in a male-dominated workplace. In return, if he's a true friend, he'll listen and really *hear* you. He'll begin to sympathize or even empathize with your situation—and maybe, in some cases, give you reasons to see the situation differently.

Just having someone to vent to helps ease the burden. But as the relationship develops, you can take it a step further: tell him what to look out for and ask him to speak up when he sees questionable behavior. Having a guy who is promoting the same opinions and views as you in the workplace moves those views from being seen as female-gender based to those shared by both genders. This approach of getting a diverse group to share your views is extremely powerful. Once you get someone on the "majority" side repeating and endorsing your agenda, your views propagate much more quickly and are not seen as divisive.

Office ally or no, there will come a time when you need to call someone out yourself. See if you can "Jay Smooth it." Jay Smooth, a.k.a. John Randolph, is the author of a well-circulated 2008 YouTube video called "How to Tell Someone They Sound Racist."[4] Though it is now more than eight years old, the fact that it is still shared frequently speaks to how useful his approach is. (His delivery can be credited as well. If you haven't already watched the video, go do it—he's entertaining.) It applies as much to sexism as to racism. Jay Smooth says, "The most important thing that you've got to do is to remember the difference between the 'what they did' conversation and the 'what they are' conversation. Those are two totally different conversations, and you need to make sure you pick the right one."

He goes on to explain that the "what they did" conversation is right because it focuses on the specific words or actions you're calling out and why. The "what they are" conversation accuses them not of saying something sexist but of being sexist. He continues, "This is the conversation you *don't* want to have because that conversation takes us away from the facts of what they did and into speculation about their motives and intentions, and those are things you can only guess at and can't ever prove, and that makes it too easy for them to derail your whole argument."

What I particularly like about the approach is that when you "Jay Smooth it," you can still give them the benefit of the doubt. You're not holding their soul in judgment or shaming them. You're questioning a specific remark and giving them a fair opportunity to examine it. Without letting anyone off the hook, it's a less emotional, lighter exchange for both parties, and it's easier to go forward from.

JOIN THE MEN'S CLUB

My friend's husband recently came home complaining that all the women in his production company had demanded to join their fantasy football league. "They're not even into sports," he complained. "They just don't want to be left out of anything."

"Of course they don't," she told him. "Stuff like Fantasy Sports that exclude women is why four of your five executive producers are men!"

"We're not trying to exclude anybody. We just want to play. Meanwhile they have no idea what they're doing and are going to bring down the game," he said.

And so it goes at male-dominated workplaces all across the land. Whether it's sports or comic books or video games, women who aren't interested naturally get left out. (In my friend's case the office came up with a solution: each of the women who was new to the game was teamed up with a male buddy to show her the ropes. Next season they'll take the training wheels off. The solution made the game more fun for everybody.)

Sometimes these acts of inclusion don't need to be as hard as we make them. My friend Kate Mitchell, the cofounder of Scale Venture Partners, had a simple strategy for joining gendered conversations. At meetings of the private equity firm where she was a partner a "male conversation" would often kick off a meeting. Half the time it might be sports oriented or at least include sports analogies. So the morning before, say, a portfolio company board meeting she'd step over the *USA Today* in the doorway of her hotel room and scan the headlines for what she privately referred to as her "sports fact," something like, "Rodriguez traded to Rangers."

Kate explains, "To make this work, I don't need to know that his first name is Alex. I don't even need to know he plays baseball. When I walk into the room, I say, 'Rodriguez was traded to the Rangers.' I never need more than that. The guys want to show me they know more than I do." That simple, thirty-second prep allowed her to be part of the chitchat in their eyes and hers. Furthermore, she was the instigator of the conversation, giving her the leadership position in casual boardroom conversation. As superficial as it was, it made a difference in getting the only woman in the room positioned to be part of the core board discussion that followed.

■ ■ ■

ALTHOUGH YOU SHOULDN'T have to become a sports enthusiast to get promoted at work, I will say this: building relationships with anyone of any gender or ethnicity or race is much easier if you're willing to open your mind and try new things. If you're surrounded by men who love, say, football, why not do a little research and give it a chance? Of course, you might already love football. But for all those women who closed their minds to the sport because they were conditioned against it, why not take a little time to learn the game? Get to know the rules, explore players' bios, go to a game, and be prepared to cheer. You might find you like it.

And if not, move on. As for me, it was pretty clear I knew nothing about American sports and didn't have much capacity or patience to learn. I never could wrap my head around how a football game that had one minute and fifty-eight seconds on the clock could still be going on ten minutes later. As a result there were plenty of events I was never invited to. But for every event I was not invited to because it was outside my interests I planned a group activity that I enjoyed a lot—a dinner, a hike, even shooting guns with our local SWAT Team—so I would never resent being left out. And because I was always visible and assertive, I began to find that any important conversation I missed eventually circled back to me, usually with a request for my input.

I'm using sports as a proxy because it's one of the most common "gendered" interests you're likely to encounter in a typical workplace. But this advice applies to any topic. The goal is to establish yourself as having an opinion that counts. Once you do that, you'll find it matters a lot less whether you're invited to every event—whether you're there or not, people want to know what you think.

MALE-FEMALE NETWORKING HACKS

If you've found that your networking has veered female as you or your colleagues have partnered off and had children, you can course correct.

Gina Bianchini has dedicated more than a decade to helping people create rewarding networks, first as the CEO of Ning, an early leader in the social networking and community space, and today as founder and CEO of Mighty Networks, a company that helps people create and run mobile interest networks. Aside from the expertise that evolves from her companies' mission, any woman who has founded two high-profile startups is a consummate expert in building and leveraging a network to accomplish a goal.

"The constraints are real," Gina says. "At marrying and family stages it becomes much more uncomfortable to network with men in the same way you can with women." The day I interviewed her Gina had just added a new hack to her repertoire. She had planned drinks with two men, and then one dropped out. Instead of canceling or facing the potential awkwardness of a one-on-one night meeting, she called him up and said, "Who else should we invite?" He suggested they invite someone she had never met. So not only did she get to meet someone new, but she also created a more socially comfortable environment for herself. This practical hack has a strong secondary benefit: meeting people in groups gets you a better return on your precious time away from home than would one-on-ones.

Gina also has advice for conferences or events that are uncomfortably male-dominated. "You don't excuse yourself—you find someone to bring to the party. That person is your wing man." This is the event version of your office ally. It's someone you trust whose presence shifts the dynamic so you feel included and safe. It doesn't need to be someone of the same sex. "It's someone where you're like, 'You're my friend. There's no vibe here whatsoever that there's a problem, and you're going to come with me to this,'" she says. "Those guys exist. They always exist. You have to look for them."

Gina herself shies away from the word ally, calling it fundamentally flawed. "Implicit in that description is women are going to help me more, and men are 'allies.' It sets up an expectation of gender-based hierarchy in who's supposed to be more helpful to you or not. It's dangerous because it serves the wrongheaded assumption that women's most loyal and natural advocates are other women. They may be, but it's not a given."

Of course, there is no such thing as gender-blind behavior when it comes to human interaction. Women's attitudes toward ourselves and others have been filtered through this lens. We need to be active in noticing and correcting its perversions where they exist. The same goes for men.

Make a conscious choice to choose the conversations and relationships you enter not on the basis of gender but rather on their importance to your goals. Meanwhile build relationships and alliances that make it impossible for anyone to ever push you out. Powering UP becomes infinitely easier when you convince the people who have the power to welcome you in.

7

Guilt and Other Challenges of Working Parenthood

I briefly considered leaving parenting out of this book. I am frustrated that women are so often asked to reflect in public and private on the consequences that their career will have or has had on their ability to parent and vice versa. I have never heard this question asked of a man. It also seemed, at first glance, as though technology was on its way to solving this perceived conflict—or at least dramatically altering the conversation—for the upcoming generation of women leaders by giving them the ability to freeze their eggs and delay childbearing until their forties. Finally, I didn't want to add to the social pressure on women to become mothers. So let me say upfront that if you're not sure whether you want kids or know absolutely that you do not want kids, I believe that these are all valid life choices.

The fact is that many women do have children, and as one woman I interviewed put it, it's almost always a gobsmack experience. There is no turning point more stark and monumental in most women's careers. Several women I spoke to told me that they hadn't thought their gender had had any effect on their professional life until the moment children were in their immediate horizon. Becoming a mother is a beautiful, empowering experience, but it is also the real Herculean challenge for working women today.

I mentioned that egg freezing is giving young women today more control over the impact of maternity on their careers. Options help, but having kids in your forties has challenges too. You're making more money (hopefully), but you also have more responsibility. It's a hard moment to suddenly introduce parenting, the equivalent of a second full-time job, into your life. This is not to say that egg freezing is a bad thing, only that it doesn't erase the challenges of having two babies—your progeny and your career—to which you would like to be able to devote yourself entirely. Changing America's business culture and the policies that govern it will help. But for those who are passionate about their careers, the tension will always be there. There are only so many hours in a day.

For all these reasons it's never too early to start to think about whether you'll parent, how you'll parent, and how you'll integrate that life with your professional one. The integration is about logistics—scheduling, leave time, child care—but it's also about identity. Reading this, you may be in a phase of life when you're more worried about how to prevent babies than how to have them. But I urge you to start chewing on these questions now.

When I raised my sons, only two in ten women were primary bread earners, according to the Pew Research Center.[1] Today the figure is four in ten. Though I was not completely immune to society's disapproval, I mostly found it easy to ignore. I had decided from a very young age that stay-at-home motherhood was simply not an option for me—not only for my own happiness but for that of any children I might have. I decided this based on my own experience as a daughter.

A reporter from *USA Today* once called to interview me for a Mother's Day feature. She wanted to know whether my mother had influenced my future career. "Yes, she certainly did," I said. "Growing up, my mother showed me every day what *not* to do and how difficult and frustrating life could be without my own income or independence."

The startled reporter politely listened to my story, a point of view on motherhood that was no doubt not easy to hear. To her credit, she included it in her article on a positive note, despite the fact that it wasn't a Hallmark-ready inspirational tale.

My mother, Selma Yeşil, was a fantastic mom, but she was mostly unhappy throughout my childhood. Growing up female in Turkey in the 1940s, life imposed many constraints on her, and without alternatives, she bitterly accepted them all. For a brief moment, through a sponsor, she had the opportunity to come to the United States for university. She would have studied medicine, but being the only daughter, she felt deeply conflicted given family responsibilities. In Turkey, then and now, as elsewhere, daughters are the assumed caregivers of aging parents. Ultimately she sacrificed her opportunity for advancement so she could stay home and support them.

Like so many women before and after her, my mother became the poster child of sacrificing her own desires to support the desires of others: her mother, her husband, her mother-in-law, her children. She had to do everything for everyone else, and she received little in return. Our appreciation and praise was never enough to overcome the pain she felt over the opportunity she sacrificed. As a child, my mother's habitual griping made me sad. I knew I wanted things to be better for me. So one of my first mantras when I learned English became "Win not whine," a phrase I picked up from my first English teacher. My mother was the cautionary tale of what I imagined might happen if I didn't reach out and seize every exciting opportunity I could find, even—or especially—those that seemed to be off-limits.

Motherhood as modeled by my mother's generation was a nonstarter for me. I believed there was another version of motherhood that would better suit me. As far back as I could remember I had wanted to have children, and I went on to become one of the first among my Stanford classmates to do it. I think that's because I had internalized my father's parenting approach. He loved being a father and made it look fun. He took time off work to take us to the beach or to come to our school to screen old Hollywood comedies for the whole student body. He organized a ten-day annual camping trip for us and fifty other teenagers and was our camp counselor. My father was able to be deeply involved in our lives and to cherish our dreams without sacrificing his own. As alienating as motherhood appeared to me, engaged fatherhood—let's just call it parenthood—was something I aspired to. And because watching my dad made me believe that having a career and having children were completely doable, I never really considered *not* having children as an option. Neither did I ever consider life without a career. My father had convinced me very early on that I should make my own money, even if I married the richest man in the world.

Neither my father nor I could have ever juggled parenthood and career with the relative ease that we did without my mother. She raised my sons as much as I did. After my father passed away, she was lonely and without purpose in Turkey, so she moved to California. When I gave birth to my first son, she moved in with us.

My mother cooked three meals a day and cared for our sons round the clock. This arrangement allowed me to jump on red-eye flights to meet with investors, take last-minute meetings on opposite coasts, and sometimes work long hours without worrying for a minute about whether my kids were being actively loved and cared for.

Although my mother loved our sons and seemed to enjoy taking them to the corner park to play, I still saw much of the same frustrated behavior I remembered from my childhood. But the story ends with a happy twist. When my sons started preschool my mother, at age sixty-three, opened her life to an entirely new experience: she got her first job. Selma Yeşil became the barista at the bakery of our local Whole Foods Market. She learned how to make cappuccinos and the exotic names of American cookies, such as snickerdoodles. The job—and the paycheck that came with it—transformed her. She blossomed in front of our eyes.

My mother never went to college, but she had been taught six languages by the private Swiss tutor who schooled her at home on the island of Buyukada until age fourteen, when she finally went to the local American high school. She was well read, knew most operas by heart, and followed world events, making her the ideal barista for the high-achieving international Stanford University crowd who frequented the store. She enjoyed the celebrity afforded by her central position behind the counter and served her customers with great enthusiasm. She so loved her job that she would often show up twenty minutes before her shift and wait outside. Soon she was charged with opening the store in Palo Alto. She was recognized all over. On any given day she seemed to have been in conversations with half the town and in half a dozen languages. For the first time in her life, slinging cappuccinos and chatting up strangers helped her feel respected and valued. I saw a marked positive change in her attitude when she took the kids to the park on Saturday afternoons. Being paid for work and recognized for even a small pursuit outside of the home made her feel validated and valued by others, and she was a much happier person for it. (Years later when my son Troy worked on Amazon's acquisition of Whole Foods, she felt proud to have contributed in her own way to this success.)

Watching my mother transform at sixty-three strengthened my conviction that for myself and many others, combining parenthood with a career makes for a happier life than seclusion in the home. It also can make us better parents—and better role models too. For those of us who want careers, I say let's stop pretending there's any alternative to finding a way to make work and motherhood a more comfortable fit. Men have always had that luxury; now it's our turn to rewrite the rules.

NO MORE MOMMY GUILT

I would have liked to think that "mommy guilt" disappeared with conical bras and those blouses with the big, smart bow tied tight at the neck. It hasn't. I have the pleasure of meeting many professional high achievers who are also new mothers. Almost without fail, when they hear about the career I had as a mother of two, they start asking questions, all of which seem to toe toward the one they are too polite to ask: *Did your sons turn out okay?*

Even today, with both of my sons happy and successful by their own measure, I recently experienced a moment of overwhelming mommy guilt. I was on a group hike, and a woman in her late twenties asked me if I was a mom. Given her young age, I immediately thought by *mom* she meant someone with kids still at home, and I answered no without thinking. She was walking faster than me, so we split. As I hiked I reflected on her question and realized she might just have been asking whether I had children at all.

Feeling the need to correct the record, I caught up with her and said, "You know, I actually am a mom. I have two grown sons." The way she looked at me, even after I had explained myself, you would think I had told her I had dumped my babies at a train station. But as awkward as that moment was, the real shaming was yet to come. Miles later on the hike I drifted into conversations with two other people who separately said, "Oh! You! You're the woman who forgot she was a mother."

This is the same cultural shaming that makes working mothers feel guilty even when they have moved heaven and earth to make sure their children are happy, healthy, and bathed in love, care, and enrichment every waking hour. It seems strange that this anxiety still exists in an age when so many women are primary breadwinners, but it is frankly an elite concern. Being a stay-at-home mom is a privilege available only to a precious few.

Heidi Zak, who had her first child in the year after she launched her company and has since had a second, is one of the most well-adjusted mom-CEOs I've ever met. She told me that in the rare moments when she feels a pang of guilt, she reminds herself of three things. First, she's tremendously lucky to be able to work at something she loves. Second, she's proud to expand the universe of female founders and add to the list of "powerful women who are doing amazing things and who aren't talking about being guilty." And third, she strongly believes her kids will appreciate having parents who teach them by example that both moms and dads do cool things professionally. "I hope in five or ten years they say, 'I love my mom. She's an awesome mom and she does something really cool.'"

I can remember how my sons proudly led their friends through bookstores to the shelf where my book *Creating the Virtual Store: Taking Your Website from Browsing to Buying* sat, with my picture on the back cover. I can also remember how happy my younger son was when the flight attendants of a United flight recognized me as the woman who starred in one of their in-flight entertainment programs, talking about electronic commerce and Internet payments on United's high-technology special program. Actually, he was most happy that they brought him handfuls of chocolates because of his "celebrity" mother. My sons also loved the free cookies that were always left over from the Friday partner meetings when I took them to the office with me on weekends to catch up on work. Having a working mother had fringe benefits.

But I can *also* remember the time I listened to my older son chatting with his classmate in the backseat as I drove them on a ski trip. They were both about thirteen, and the classmate's mother was the CEO of a hot e-commerce company. If you've served as a chauffeur to children, you might have noticed that they talk as though they're alone in a driverless vehicle. You hear some great stuff, and in this case I listened to them planning their future romantic lives. They were definitely going to marry, and when they did, they agreed, it would be to wives who were home all the time and were reliable cooks, unlike their own mothers. They also bemoaned how long it took their own mothers to do the tasks they asked them to—if they did them at all.

If our culture doesn't do its job to make you feel guilty about being ambitious, at some point your kids will. My heart fell out that day in the car. But trust me: when a three- or thirteen-year-old tells you,

"You're ruining my life!" it shouldn't be mistaken as actionable life or career advice. If I have any complaint these days from my sons, it wasn't that I wasn't present *enough* in their lives but, if anything, *too* present in terms of my expectations for their studies and their future. I am a high achiever, and I expected my sons to be too. Fortunately for everybody, neither of them ran off and joined the circus.

SHAPING YOUR CAREER
AND YOUR PARENTING TOGETHER

As you've probably heard, if you have not yet experienced it yourself, it's not easy to power UP as a committed parent in the United States, where business and culture are so invested in rapid growth. It's even harder in Silicon Valley, where every company is in a race to ship first and where, in large part, men with spouses who take the domestic lead, if not the entire burden, still write the rules of professional engagement.

One time I was about to be interviewed for a live technology news broadcast. It was minutes before we went on the air, and the reporter and I were seated in our chairs next to each other. The reporter noticed me jotting things down on a small notepad and asked if I was preparing my answers, reminding me that I could not read anything off my pad while filming. I showed him what I was writing. When he saw it he laughed. "I've never had anyone about to go on live TV writing their grocery list!" he said.

Maybe I was the first working mother he had as a guest. "It's my next stop after your show," I said. "When else am I going to write it?"

Even with a full-time grandma at home, my children influenced my career choices from the moment they were born. That said, I never thought of the opportunities that I turned down as being sacrifices. I always believed I could find alternatives that would suit our family *and* satisfy me professionally.

My children were the reason I turned down a job at Apple for the *second* time. (As I mentioned in Chapter 1, I turned them down the first time because a professor advised me against working for a technology company that had a fruit for its name.) Steve Jobs had just made his big comeback to Apple and was considering me as his vice president of marketing. After spending a few days with him at his office, brainstorming around Apple's ad campaign and working on a potential PR strategy, he asked me to continue working over the weekend.

Sure, I said.

I went over early Saturday, and we had a terrific day working together, finally breaking around eight at night. Before I left he said, "Hey, today was great. Let's work together again tomorrow?" I agreed and was again working with him from morning to late at night. It was exhilarating and exhausting. Needless to say, I didn't see my children, then seven and nine, at all that weekend.

Monday came, and Steve offered me the opportunity to join Apple and to continue to work with him. I smiled and told him how honored I felt. Then I said, "But this job isn't for me."

Steve was shocked. "But didn't you have fun? Isn't this incredible?" he wanted to know.

Of course, I did, and it was. But I had a family and responsibilities outside of work, and I suspected that the way we worked that weekend was the way I would work with him going forward. There was no way that would be sustainable for me. Though technically the support of my mother and babysitter made seven-day work weeks *possible*, it wasn't what I wanted.

FAMILY SATURDAYS AT THE OFFICE

Throughout my career I have had to go into the office on weekends, and I'd often need to bring my boys with me. When I had to work on a sunny day that would have been perfect for a beach outing or a trip to the park, I needed a way to make cold, quiet office time more appealing.

We did not have TV at home because I was at work for long hours and did not want them watching it all that time. So when I started founding companies when my children were three and five, I got a TV for my office conference room. Going to work with Mom on a Saturday went from being a punishment to a treat, a day they chose when and how much TV to watch. I also had a lot of toys in the office that hadn't worn out their novelty like the ones at home. Add a cookie or two from the office kitchen, and a weekend office day became a very fun activity.

So I turned Steve Jobs down and never looked back. Someone recently asked me if I regretted that decision. As a matter of practice, I don't "do regret" because it's a waste of energy. What I took away from Steve's offer was positive: confirmation of my skills and my commitment to choose a job that fit my own needs.

If you're someone who cares about being home at 6:30 to have dinner with your kids and you work in an organization where the real work and face time happen in the late hours of the evening, you're going to feel like an outsider and fall behind. Look for a company that positions you to thrive given your limitations. I've always believed that your most important "marriage" in terms of making your career work is the professional cohort you choose, whether that's a company or your business partners. If you choose an environment that's in conflict with your needs, you'll feel you're being forced to blow up your life to accommodate your work, an uncomfortable arrangement that makes you feel victimized instead of in control of your choices. You might start to feel like you're trying to do everything and succeeding at nothing.

That feeling of being pulled apart has given rise to a widely accepted notion that parenthood and career can only be in tension with each other. Do well at one, and you're doing it at the expense of the other. In fact, parenthood can make you a better, more effective, more ambitious professional than before. Lynn Perkins of UrbanSitter can rattle off a laundry list of ways that her kids have enhanced her professional life. First of all, she owes the birth of UrbanSitter to the birth of her children. (I'll come back to that story later.) Lynn also told me that despite having fewer hours for work, as a mother she still gets more done because she's become so good at prioritizing her attention and managing her time. "It's amazing," she told me. "I look back and I think, what did I do in my twenties? When I woke up on a Saturday morning I went out for brunch, and I thought 9 a.m. was early. Now by nine I've done twenty things!"

Lynn was once the kind of worker whose brain was churning 24/7, whether she was at her desk or on her couch. Today she gives her kids her full attention when she walks in the door after a day of work. But doing so has had an unexpected benefit. "You know how sometimes you actually come up with good ideas when you're not thinking about your work? A forced break is really, really a good thing," she says. Finally, she says, the fact that she stays home in the evenings after her kids go to bed at 7:30 means she's actually more likely to do evening work than she'd be if she had a swinging, out-on-the-town social life.

The key is finding a way to shape your work life and your family schedule together. For many that means exploring flextime or working at home. Even in the most supportive environment you'll need to actively advocate for yourself. Before you even ask, make sure you've thought through the specifics as carefully as you would any project that crosses your desk. As always with your career, you need to be ready to sell the future. First, ask yourself if you could be truly effective in your position if you were home five days a week. If that seems untenable, what about two or three? If you are going to propose working from home, be convinced that you will be able to have an environment and the elements that will allow you to win at your job.

Then sift through all the details:

▪ Does HR have existing policies?

▪ Do you have a dedicated office space at home, or can you create one?

▪ What tools would you use to make yourself accessible for conversations and check-ins?

▪ How will you measure your effectiveness as an at-home employee?

▪ How long will you want to work at home or with flexible hours?

Do not pitch a work schedule to your boss until you are fully convinced that you can make it a wild success. When you meet to ask for any kind of change in your work pattern you should have a written plan that lays out what you might call the "business case" for what you're proposing. It should be clear that you have thought through the plan as someone who has the best interests of the company in mind. Explain and convince your boss that your plan is going to make the company more successful than if you worked from the office every day. Clearly articulate and justify the reasons—from your employer's point of view, not your personal one.

There's a danger, of course, to stepping physically away from the office or limiting your facetime. Your colleagues, even those with the best intent, may wrongly assume that your priorities have shifted to the home and offer the most challenging, career-advancing assignments to the childless desk jockey who goes home late. You can also lose opportunities simply by being out of sight, out of mind. The women I know who have been most successful have taken steps to amplify their presence when they reduce their face time, from maternity leave forward. A few tips:

1. **TAKE A "VISIBLE" PARENTAL LEAVE.** When Anna Sale, the host of WNYC's *Sex, Death, and Money* podcast, took four months off for the birth of her first child, she told *New York* magazine she was taking a "visible" leave.[2] While wanting to protect most of her time for her new infant, she participated in each episode by calling in and having a short on-air chat with the guest host. She wanted to create the sense that "maternity leave is happening for Anna, but she's still living and breathing and a real person."

2. **SET CLEAR PRIORITIES WITH YOUR BOSS.** Before and after maternity leave let your boss know that although your work schedule is changing, your dedication is not. If you don't make

this clear, he or she might assume they're doing you a favor by taking your name out of the hat for new projects and assignments. When talking about a shift to satellite or flextime work, make sure you have clear performance goals that you can use to measure how well the new arrangement is working. And be sure to work longer hours than those having to commute to work regularly, showing up on the company chat channel early and being present into the late hours as well as turning emails and requests around faster than ever. Increasing your productivity and giving more to the company, not less, is the only way to make this new arrangement successful.

3. **BE STRATEGIC ABOUT FACE TIME.** Know which meetings are okay to phone in and which require your presence. Make sure that the hours you're in the office aren't just face time but in-your-face time. Maximize the opportunity to sit down with people. Schedule lots of time for internal networking. If you start feeling like you are being forgotten or passed over, listen to your instincts: you are probably right. Either be ready to accept these negative consequences or be ready to go back to physically reporting into work daily.

4. **RECRUIT EYES AND EARS.** Some of the most important conversations in an office are spontaneous and informal. Ask someone you trust—and who is plugged into the informal communication network—to be your eyes and ears in those moments to keep you up to date on those things you won't learn from email or meetings. Check in regularly, make them your ally, and reciprocate whenever possible in pushing both your careers forward.

Another question I get a lot: When do I share the news? Tell your boss or your investors you're pregnant the moment you have figured out what you want and have translated it into a strong, specific plan for the business. Think of it this way: when you meet with your boss, you're not sharing the news—you're sharing the plan.

In other words, your meeting with your boss should never be the in-person equivalent of sending out a birth announcement. Although the news is joyous for you (hopefully), it may be much more ambiguous for your boss. They may share your joy and encourage your leave time, but you've given them a management challenge to solve.

So why not solve the problem for them? This will make the news more comfortable for your boss and more importantly, gives you the most control over developing a plan for leaving and for coming back that works for you. Think through questions like How much time do I want to take off, and starting when? How do I want my job to change when I'm back? Who will cover me?

Of course, the answer to some of these questions may change over time, particularly if it's your first pregnancy. Your body and the baby's may also throw some curve balls that turn "the plan" upside down. But you know what? That's life. Your only responsibility is to do the best job you can to create a plan that works for you and your business. If you don't, someone else will, and you may not like their plan.

That said, more and more companies are learning that to attract the best talent, they need an approach to pregnancy and parenting that's more supportive to parents, and particularly to mothers, than most have in place today. Tanja Omeze, the intrapreneur and digital analytics whiz we profiled earlier, was shocked and surprised when her boss at Amazon told her she'd be receiving a full paid maternity leave. She had arrived in her new position five months pregnant and announced the pregnancy after a month on the job. She assumed she'd need more tenure to get the benefit. Not only that, when her son Jace ended up coming two months early and spending two weeks in the NICU, Tanja says her boss and HR contact moved heaven and earth to accommodate the unique needs of her delivery.

Companies who go out of their way to accommodate moms do exist—but we're a long way from everyone receiving those benefits as a matter of policy. Most people need to fight tooth and nail for them and be both resourceful and creative about blending work and motherhood. It's these moments when knowing how to power UP is more important than ever.

FAMILY LEAVE AND
THE CO-PARENTING UNICORN

Let's all adopt the language—and implicit expectation—of *family leave*. If we want to be on equal footing in the workplace, we cannot think *maternity leave* anymore. Mothers need physical recovery time, but in this era of breast pumps, fathers can be primary caregivers very early. And family leave isn't just for parents but also for people (who today are disproportionately female) caring for aging family members.

Laws and policies alone won't resolve gender bias around issues of maternity. If only women stay home to care for infants, employers will continue to see women in childbearing years as a risky class of employees. This unintended consequence will result in women not having the same opportunities to power UP, regardless of what the law says.

That's why the next major leap toward workplace parity starts at home. The more that parents make these decisions together, according to their unique needs, the stronger we'll be—at home, at work, and in the ever-growing overlapping space between them.

Gender-neutral, family-friendly policies don't necessarily level the playing field—in fact, they can make the problem even worse. That was the finding of economists who studied several universities that offered extensions on tenure review for both mothers and fathers. "The policies led to a 19 percentage-point rise in the probability that a male economist would earn tenure at his first job. In contrast, women's chances of gaining tenure fell by 22 percentage points," the *New York Times* reported.[3] Men who took advantage of the policy increased their research and publishing output significantly. The women did not. The study's authors speculated that this was because the women still carried the lion's share of the parenting burden.

Mothers who have partners need to encourage them to take advantage of family leave policies. If more men raise their hands to stay home after the birth of a child, norms will eventually shift. With parity in family leave, opportunities will increase for everyone.

Meaghan Rose, the founder of Rocksbox, a successful jewelry subscription company, decided to start her company and have her first child all at the same time. "The beginning was hard. I had to go back very quickly after my son was born because the company didn't yet have the support to carry on without me." Despite the challenges, Rose says it was all worthwhile. "I knew it would be tough at times, but it is also wonderful. I think it's important for women to hear that it is possible to have your own company and have kids—and it is in fact incredibly rewarding."

What Utopia Looks Like

For a kind of fantasy snapshot of what the future of a family-supportive workplace might look like, turn to Rent the Runway, where 80 percent of the executive management is women. The policy at Rent the Runway starts with twelve weeks of paid leave, CEO Jennifer Hyman tells me. It is open to mothers and fathers of both biological and adopted children. In months four and five after becoming parents, workers have the option to return part time, three days a week, at 100 percent of their salary, or they can take additional unpaid leave without endangering their jobs. Do not count on your future employer offering these benefits. Remember: this is utopia. But it is nice to know it exists.

Rose says her husband, who also has an intense job, "feels the responsibility of being a parent as much as I do. Not out of obligation but because he wants to be present in our son's life," she says. But the two sometimes feel like they're fighting the current. Rose observes that the gender-bias mentality for child care starts very early in our society, going back to children's books. "Most children's books focus on 'mommy and me.' I have a hard time finding a 'daddy and me' book to read to my eighteen-month-old son."

▪ ▪ ▪

TRUE 50/50 CO-PARENTING, for most women, is still a magical unicorn, not an everyday reality. The women I know who have partners who truly share the parenting and household responsibilities didn't win these enlightened men in a lottery; they sat down together and did the work: serious, conscientious, sometimes even contentious discussions before the baby came to figure out how the labor would be divvied up. Of course, not every couple needs or wants a 50/50 split, but every couple should have the discussion. If they don't, statistically women carry the brunt, even when both parents work.

Julia Hartz is one of the few women I've spoken who says she and her husband truly share the responsibilities of home and family 50/50. Maybe it's because they've done it so long in a business context: together, Julia and her husband founded Eventbrite, the well-known event ticketing and management platform. From 2006 until 2016 Kevin Hartz was the company's CEO. Since April 2016 Julia has worn the hat—"We almost switched places, in a way," she says.

Becoming CEO was, in fact, a major shift for Julia, requiring both a surge of confidence and a willingness to rethink her professional identity. First she wasn't sure she was ready for the role, despite tremendous support from everyone at Eventbrite. And once she was officially CEO, she found herself up late the first night after the board's decision, asking Kevin to "name one loveable female CEO." (His answer? "*You.*")

Those anxieties faded quickly as she did the job and found out that, yes, she was cut out not just to be a CEO but to be a very good one—and yes, she could be lovable too. Then and now she and Kevin, whatever their formal titles, have always been partners on the same team. "We have built our marriage and our parenthood under the auspices of being cofounders," she told me. "Yes, I birthed the children and took a longer leave after them, but other than that we've had complete parity on how we work and how we handle domestic duties.

Julia and Kevin are the unicorn.

The two carefully worked through their rules of engagement as fellow founders and parents. She attributes their success to both intention and follow-through. When problems come up, they "problem solve and life hack together."

Despite their equal status, Julia nevertheless catches herself wanting to give him more credit for his contribution than she does for her own. "Oh my gosh, he's a feminist and look how supportive he is. But actually, according to our own operating rules, it's inappropriate for me to be giving him more credit," she says. Brava to that.

The stigma is real. Let's support and encourage our dads and stop berating those moms who *opt* for short leaves. We all need to question established norms and policies that view childrearing as gendered responsibility. If you think that is decades away, here is a case that may change your mind. GoldieBlox, a leading company in children's educational toys and media, didn't have a formal family leave policy until the first time an employee asked to take a leave due to childbirth—and as it happened, that employee was a man. Now Debbie Sterling, the CEO of GoldieBlox, is due to have her first child in the fall of 2016. "My husband and I have not yet decided how much leave we will take," says Sterling, "It will depend on how I am feeling and the needs of the business. We will play it by ear."

Now, how do you deal with life as a single mom with three little kids, working at a job that pays hourly—let alone worry about advancing your career? The short answer is you make it work. In fact, millions of women make it work every day. The key is finding a supportive community, a supportive company, and a supportive boss. Take any job you can, but keep interviewing to trade up until you find a company and a boss who is supportive. Some larger companies even have on-site childcare, and others have flexible hours. And remember, the most intense part of childrearing is only ten years, while your career is forty-five or more. Don't get discouraged if you cannot advance as quickly as you want during your childrearing years. You have years ahead of you, and with the right motivation and hard work, you will be able to achieve your dreams, if not today, once the kids are situated at school or off to college.

WHEN PARENTHOOD
MAKES ENTREPRENEURS OF EMPLOYEES

The culture of the American workplace of the twentieth century was built around the expectation that there was a wife at home to cook, clean, and take care of the children. That's rarely the case anymore, and both women and men are hurting because of it. And because women statistically still take on more household responsibilities than men, those of us who are working outside the home as well are hurting more.

For a decade American women's participation in the workforce has trended negative. Sixty-one percent of nonworking women cite family responsibilities as the reason, according to the *New York Times* in December 2015. In a 2016 McKinsey/LeanIn study, fear of balancing work and family responsibilities was listed by more women (42 percent) than any other reason for not wanting to become a top executive. The same percentage of men said work-family balance kept them from seeking a senior role.

I'm one of many women who turned to entrepreneurship as an answer—a world where I worked as hard or harder than ever before but owned my schedule for the most part. Let's not pretend this is a path that's easy, particularly for a single parent or anyone of modest means. All the entrepreneurs I met who were juggling foundership with young children were married and in a financial position to afford full-time nannies. As for me, the fact that my husband worked, we lived frugally, and we had an on-site caregiver who was a grandmother, not an employee, made it possible for me to invest in myself as an entrepreneur by working the equivalent of full-time work for several years without any pay.

Theresia Gouw is a venture capitalist who works with new CEOs every day as the cofounder of Aspect Ventures with Jennifer Fonstad. Aspect is focused on investing during a company's Series A round, the first institutional investment a company receives. Theresia points out that the best years in your life to start a company coincide with the best years of your life to have a child. "Can you handle both? The answer depends on how much uncertainty you can live with. Both experiences push you into the unknown, where you cannot have clear visibility to what the future will bring," she says.

The good news is that a new generation of women founders are creating companies with HR policies and culture that respect that employees have responsibilities outside the office. Lynn Perkins of UrbanSitter is one of them. Lynn's most recent entrepreneurship story starts very typically: when kids made balancing two demanding careers impossible, she was the spouse to quit her job.

She and her husband were both working full time, with two-and-a-half-year-old twins at home. Her husband traveled frequently for work, while she traveled occasionally. She worked for a company that flipped hotels in California; they would buy, say, a Best Western in Venice Beach, give it a hip redesign, boost room rates, and then sell it.

The situation was working well until a national group acquired the company, and she would need to be traveling around the United States instead of making the occasional day trip. And so she quit, despite liking the job. She decided to take a few months off to figure out her next step, "one of the few times in life I decided to just go with the flow," she said.

Although Lynn had founded a tech startup earlier in her career, she didn't quit with the intention of starting something on her own. And yet, after quitting in September, by Thanksgiving she had not just hatched a great idea with cofounder Andrea Barrett—a site that used social networks to help parents find well-matched, quality babysitters—but also recruited an engineer, the husband of a friend, to start working with her on building it. By January they were well on their way to developing UrbanSitter.

When it came time to recruit engineers, Lynn worried that in go-go-go Silicon Valley she'd have trouble finding people to work at a company whose founders were all parents. Their work culture wasn't "coming to work at noon and playing ping-pong until 2 a.m." It was get in, do the work, and get out by five to be home with their families. It turned out that there were plenty of really good engineers who had kids and were delighted by an alternative to the all-night hero coding that plenty of Valley companies encouraged. Says Lynn, "I've realized that being at a startup is not really a sprint. It's like a half-marathon. You don't want people to totally burn out. I love that here you don't feel like you have to creep out so that no one sees you leaving at five." At UrbanSitter most employees are parents, but even those who don't have kids appreciate the life balance embedded in the culture of the company. After all, any other position would be incoherent for a company whose mission is to put kids' care first.

As more women like Lynn power their way to the top, the more opportunity other women will have to experience parenthood the way fathers always have: as personally joyful and fulfilling, with a professional benefit as well. Our children are ultimately an irrepressible source of power. They inspire us to bring our best to work, to support them, and to make them proud.

8

Quitting, Failing, Reentry, and Rebirth

In 2004 Salesforce went public, selling 10 million shares of stock for $110 million dollars. By closing bell the day of the initial public offering (IPO) the stock price was up more than 55 percent. It was a wild endorsement of everything the developers, the sales and customer success folks, the founders, the board, and everyone on the team had worked so hard for. Customers loved us, and revenue was growing steadily. Now armed with IPO cash, the company had significant resources to invest in its next major stage of growth. As the company's first board member, I was proud and excited to play my part in this next phase.

I got to enjoy this peak period for a while. And then everything changed. There comes a point in everyone's career when life—be it birth, death, or simply our health—intercedes in our careful professional planning. Just as I was really starting to enjoy this new period of growth, a health issue I had been grappling with got worse. I faced the potential that it would become something chronic and seriously debilitating.

> There comes a point in everyone's career when life—
> be it birth, death, or simply our health—intercedes
> in our careful professional planning.

There were a lot of unknowns when I met with my doctor, but as happens all too often, all I could hear was the worst-case scenario. To me, my doctor's recommendation to cut back my workload significantly was almost as scary as the prognosis. After all, I had worked so hard to build my career. Now I was supposed to walk away just as all the hard work was paying off?

Cutting back work meant making difficult choices, and the most difficult was leaving the board of Salesforce. Salesforce took the lion's share of my time and attention, and I couldn't sustain that level of productivity and expect to stay healthy.

I asked Marc Benioff to meet me right away for breakfast. "I need to leave the board," I told him. It was a sad day for both of us. He was disappointed and concerned, but I didn't leave him any room for questioning.

This seemed to be the right choice at the time, but now I question that "all or nothing" approach. The worst-case scenario didn't happen, and I didn't build that possibility into my plan. What had seemed like a morbid death sentence at the time turned out to be a manageable health problem. And over time I developed new strategies and became comfortable with my new normal. Two big misses contributed to my decision.

First, I failed to go to others for counsel. Today my first rule of quitting is this: never, ever throw in the towel on anything without talking it over with several people you trust who can offer diverse perspectives. At the time I didn't speak to anyone other than my husband who, like me, was processing the news emotionally. Neither of us could apply critical judgment to the question of what would come next.

Second, I made a mistake that women make all the time: I thought I had to be perfect and that nothing below perfect was acceptable. Specifically, I thought that anything less than a clean bill of health meant it would be irresponsible to hold a board seat. Rather than dealing with problems as they developed, I became terrified and panicked, and I made a hasty decision.

Lynn Perkins of UrbanSitter told me a story that similarly emphasizes how hard we women are on ourselves when it comes to balancing our commitments. A week after taking in a $6 million round of investment in 2012, Lynn learned she was pregnant. The thought of telling her investors was agonizing. Would they think they had made a $6 million mistake? Or that she hadn't been forthcoming about her pregnancy during the fundraising? She was so nervous about the conversation that she went to them one-on-one with a carefully prepared and rehearsed speech, hammering home the message that any impact on the business would be short term.

Their reaction shocked her. Instead of expressing concern about the business impact or her seriousness as a CEO, they congratulated her. "You're probably planning to come back right away.

Make sure you take some time off," one said. (If only women throughout the workforce food chain got such a response.) When she explained she had been worried about how this would affect their perception of her and her business, they shook their heads and shared stories about the crazy things other CEOs in their portfolio companies had done.

"One told a story about a CEO who had suddenly announced he was taking an eight-week sailing trip to 'find himself' in the middle of an important phase of his company's growth," says Lynn. "So to me this investor says, 'You're asking to take a few weeks off to have a kid? That's nothing! You'll use your own product! It's fabulous.'"

Although not every investor or boss will react so beautifully, you increase your chances by presenting the topic exactly the way Lynn and so many successful future mothers have: "I'm pregnant. Here's the timeline and the plan for how I'm going to make 100 percent sure it doesn't slow down our progress." Be specific in your plan, and present it not just from your point of view but also from that of your team's.

Perfectionism might be inborn for some, but overall women seem to be saddled with it more than men. If that's the case, it's not because we're crazy but because we are conditioned. As my friend Patti Hart, who has survived critical attacks several times as a CEO and leader, says, "Women have a tendency to be much more highly scrutinized. Everyone looks for the blemish in a woman, both physically and figuratively. It's harder for women to push through because we have this feeling that we have to be so perfect in everything we do."

In Chapter 6 I mentioned my former habit of "Magdalena bashing." Thank goodness for colleagues who were always willing to show me the gap between my impossible expectations for myself and the reality of what any human being could reasonably contribute. Later, building the Salesforce product helped me embrace the golden rule of Good Enough. To offer a highly effective customer relationship management product for a very small percentage of our competitors' price we had to figure out the 20 percent of the functionality that really mattered to users. These days I apply the rule of Good Enough to most things that cross my desk.

Perfectionism never serves us. Of course, for the perfectionist herself, accepting this truth feels like a cheap excuse for accepting sloppiness, error, and even failure. Aside from our own standards, we are rightfully afraid of being judged. But should we really care so much about other people's opinions about us and our work? I've always found my own opinion to carry much more influence on my outcomes than others' opinions. Confidence trumps perfection every time.

We must give ourselves latitude to screw up. Otherwise we become so anxious that we can't do our best work. Likewise, if we make our decisions guided by others' priorities or beliefs about the "proper" way to do things, we shortchange not just our careers but our entire lives as well.

Most of us are far more anxious than we should be about our life's inevitable coughs and sputters. When I asked a handful of accomplished senior women what they would change about how they handled their careers, they unanimously said, "Worry less!"

Even the most successful, "perfect" career has breaks, those times when we either opt out or are opted out against our will. If we can leave our perfectionism behind, we can make decisions—or accept the decisions that others make for us—with so much less fear while owning the results.

BREAKS ARE NOT BLEMISHES

One of the earliest lessons I received in résumé writing was to "mind the gap"—any period of time that couldn't be neatly stamped with a job title and list of duties. Whether voluntary or forced, a leave of absence from the professional world was seen as dubious, possibly flaky. Why would any skilled, capable, mentally sound go-getter take a break from a paycheck?

Thankfully that advice has become outmoded quickly, along with so much else. The acceptable modern résumé can include a jitterbug of different companies, experiences, and yes, breaks. What would have looked like professional schizophrenia or lack of commitment to employers thirty years ago today seems custom-tailored to an increasingly entrepreneurial world in the new economy. As maternity leave continues its shift to family leave and men join women in taking time off to care for the very young and the very old, personal leave will become much less stigmatized. (And while we're clearing outdated dictums, let's also toss out the notion that "life has no second acts.") Even an unwelcome period of unemployment can become a success story if it is embraced as such.

Patti Hart is a consummate glass breaker. For more than fifteen years she has served in CEO roles for heavy-hitting technology and communications companies such as DirectTV Broadband and Pinnacle Systems and in director and board roles for companies like Yahoo. Most recently she served as the CEO of International Game Technology, where she brought technology chops to the male-dominated corporate world of slots and video gaming machines in Las Vegas, Macau, Monte Carlo, and all over the world.

Patti, who has hired and fired many executives, is a strong advocate of career breaks. She says that some of the best executives she's worked with are the ones coming back after downtime. They're refreshed, they're creative, and they're committed. She sees time off as a positive and urges others to adopt the same frame of mind.

"Taking time off isn't a blemish on your record. Different stages of life deliver you different things," says Patti. "Stop thinking about time off as *I stopped doing* and start to think about it as *I did different things*. You can be a runner and not have to run every day for the rest of your life."

Whether you take time off for kids or volunteer work or a creative passion, the key, according to Patti, is thinking about it as an investment. Be able to articulate both to yourself and others how your "gap" has changed you. Find answers to questions such as *How did I recharge? What did I learn? How am I going to do things differently? Why am I a better professional today than before?*

Despite her impressive serial track record of top leadership roles, Patti's own résumé has a gap or two, not to mention some high-profile blowups. In her midforties, after spending a year leading AT&T's Excite@Home broadband network through a painful bankruptcy, she decided to take a year to "live in Paris and just do nothing." Her choice to go abroad was driven by a desire to make herself as vulnerable as possible, where she could peel away her familiar identities (mom, CEO, boss) and see what remained. The period was personally transformative, and eighteen months later she hit the ground running in a new CEO role at Pinnacle Systems.

When she left Pinnacle she took another break. She spent three years serving on various public, private, and nonprofit boards, what's sometimes called a *portfolio career*. During this time she learned how to exert influence without formal authority but instead through the quality of her ideas and information and how she presented them. Working with nonprofits was a chance to learn while serving others.

When she took her next CEO role at IGT she had new appreciation for the separation between board chairman and CEO, allowing her to use her board much more effectively than ever before.

A BLUEPRINT FOR REENTRY

The secret to owning your career even in those times when you step out of it is actually very simple: you may leave your job, but you never leave your community.

When Patti talks about her year in Paris it quickly becomes clear that there's more to the art of successful time off than reframing. Her year of "doing nothing" included almost daily coffees, lunches, and dinners—in Paris but also in London and New York—during personal trips that she booked up with meetings. She knew she wasn't making a permanent exit, so she needed to keep her network—what she calls "the connective tissue" of her professional life—healthy and strong. These are the people who will help when it comes time to plan and realize a reentry. "The network is what it all comes down to," says Patti.

Your network is equally the answer to managing the most practical challenge of time off, especially in technology: the danger of losing your knowledge edge as the landscape changes. Actually, this could equally be seen as a real *opportunity* of time off, since those who are actively employed don't have the distance they need to look forward and prepare for the next big thing.

During Patti's sabbatical the conversations at all those breakfasts didn't just oxygenate her network; they kept her knowledge fresh. As she puts it, "You have to know what's going on out there in the world. You can't just do that by reading a newspaper every day or a blog or whatever your information source is." Talking to people is how we separate signal from noise—so important when you are directing your own learning progression.

During some extended time off after the failure of my consulting business and the birth of my second son, I knew my own expertise needed a refresh if I was going to resume my career as a technologist. I was out of the loop. So once I felt recovered and ready to step back into my professional life, I dedicated six months to making myself an expert in what I had identified as the next wave, the burgeoning—yet still almost nonexistent—commercial Internet space. I completed the very first Internet user study that I mentioned earlier, which led to an opportunity to share the findings as a presenter at the first-ever commercial Internet conference.

I also spent countless hours researching the space and getting to know all the players. Like Patti, I booked my calendar with meetings, learning firsthand the state of the Internet at the time and figuring out who the main players were, what technologies were currently being used, what could be done better, and where the future demand would come from. This was all in service of searching for gaps I might fill. When I was introduced to Dan Lynch, my CV held no recent job title, but what it described was something much more useful to him. I had spent the previous six months investing in a crash course on exactly the knowledge he needed from the person who would be his partner in opening the Internet beyond research, academia, and government.

Now you might read about my experience and say, "Great, but who can afford six months of investment in their career?" No doubt, I had my husband's income to support us and my mother to care for my sons. And yet the truth is that many people find themselves in job searches that exceed six months. Inevitably a lot of that time gets wasted. This idea of focused investment is not just a useful frame to fight off the helplessness or hopelessness of a search; it can also be the difference between being a hot commodity and being passed over. And though I took on my professional development with a fever pitch, it doesn't need to be all or nothing.

The real bottom line is that whether your break is a few weeks or a few years, chosen or forced upon you, you need to find a way to maintain a connection with your field and the people in it. If you are choosing to change industries, you'll need to make a true study of the industry you want to enter, with an eye on what specific expertise you could develop. It doesn't require booking your calendar full, which for most people isn't an option; what it does require is some thoughtful evaluation so you can carve out space while setting boundaries. Answer questions such as

▌ **WHO IS IT MOST IMPORTANT TO KEEP UP WITH?** Favor quality over quantity. Prioritize contacts who tend to offer good topical intelligence and those who are connected to future opportunities.

▌ **HOW MANY MEETINGS OR CALLS A MONTH?** If you're taking time off, it's for a reason. Keeping your foot in the door is a secondary priority and with clear boundaries, will remain so.

▌ **HOW CAN YOU MAXIMIZE PRECIOUS TIME AWAY FROM HOME?** Sometimes one-on-one meetings are important, but attending a conference might allow you to catch up with a handful of people quickly.

▌ **WHAT ONE OR TWO RESOURCES CAN YOU TAP TO STAY IN THE LOOP?** You can't and shouldn't read everything. Choose carefully, and focus on where you can quickly become an expert.

When you're ready to do the full-courtpress version of reentry, don't despair. You absolutely can reinvent, reeducate, and refocus yourself, even after years on the bench.

DISASTER RECOVERY

For more evidence that a career can weather not just a long gap but also one precipitated by disaster, look no further than Julie Wainwright. Julie is the sixty-year-old CEO of a company I invested in, TheRealReal.com, an online consignment shop specializing in authenticated luxury goods. By selling designer wares culled from the closets of people like Marissa Mayer and Khloe Kardashian, the company topped $200 million in revenue in 2015 and doubled that in 2016. In short, Julie's venture has been a phenomenal success—one that came after a ten-year-plus gap.

Rewind to 2000. For those who weren't around or don't remember, that was the year the dot-com bubble burst. Julie was the CEO of Pets.com, an online pet retail company and one of the most high-profile dot-com ventures. A multimillion-dollar advertising and PR campaign had splashed its now-notorious sock puppet mascot across every media outlet in the country, including the *Today* show and the televised Macy's Thanksgiving Day Parade.

When the markets tanked and investment capital dried up, Pets.com immediately went bust, as did so many other dot-coms. For every glowing news article that had been written in its ascendency, there were now four deriding its expensive, embarrassing failure. Julie, as its figurehead, became the whipping girl for the folly and excess of an entire industry. She couldn't leave the house without being accosted by reporters, and in the Bay Area she was recognizable enough that people would stop her on the street and at events to ridicule her.

"People were writing articles about how I was the dumbest CEO they'd ever seen," says Julie. "To this day there are still people who want to meet me because I'm, like, the biggest failure story ever. Actually, Pets.com wasn't, but people didn't want to hear that story."

Her personal life offered no relief. The day Pets.com imploded she had to lay off most of her workforce, an incredibly painful experience for any CEO. The morning of the company announcement her husband asked her for a divorce—the stress was too much for him to bear. Adding to her personal struggles, "We had kind of forgotten to have kids," says Julie. Then forty-one, she was suddenly thrown into angst about whether she could or should conceive on her own. (Ultimately she did not.) Some of her closest friends weren't much help either. They seemed to be too caught up in the headlines to offer real encouragement, either personally or professionally.

"All those things collided in a pretty bad stew," she says. For a while she wallowed. She was paralyzed by an emotional and psychological low like nothing she had ever experienced. Thanks to savings and severance, she had a long runway before she needed to work—a blessing and a curse because simple economics can be a compelling force to pull yourself together.

After months of reclusion she finally decided that whatever else happened, she was done wallowing. "I just made up my mind. If I let what happened define me, I would be dead. And I was too young to die," she says.

Regardless of whether you ever find yourself in total professional freefall as Julie did, you will almost certainly experience missteps, failures, and criticism. You may one day get downsized or fired or need to close down a business. Julie's experience offers great insight for navigating those times.

How did Julie pull it back?

■ ■ ■

FIRST, SHE DECIDED TO GO HIGH. Julie started to suspect that her personal devastation, along with the degree of public scorn, might be amplified because she was a woman experiencing the fall. She thought about all the men she knew who had had businesses bust. They seemed to be like cats with nine lives, as Patti Hart likes to say, and they often seem to fall on all fours. Julie recalls thinking, "Their reaction to those failures was like, 'So what?' It was water off their back. So I said, okay, I've got to get some of that or this will kill me."

As Michelle Obama famously said, "When they go low, we go high." When people made cruel remarks, Julie stopped engaging. She stopped taking it personally. She began to notice that when people are really vicious, it's rarely about you—they're fighting their own painful battle.

She also took stock of own career. She reminded herself that Pets. com was just two years of a twenty-year career that was otherwise incredibly successful: "I knew who I was, not what people were saying about me. I reconnected with that."

■ ■ ■

SHE WIDENED HER PERSPECTIVE. When disaster hits, it helps to get out of your bubble. Julie started spending weekends out of town, heading down to LA where "nobody cared." Of course, broadening perspective doesn't always require a physical departure; it could mean taking up new activities or resuming old ones, for example.

In *Reboot: My Five Life-Changing Mistakes . . . And How I Moved On*, Julie talks about how she reopened the aperture of her own identity. She came to realize how narrowly she had defined herself on two pillars before the crash: a smart woman who could figure anything out and a married woman. Once "smart" and "married" were each scratched from her public persona, she realized that her reliance on these adjectives to measure her personal worth had "left no room for me to be just a person, who accepted my own humanness."

And so she began to reconnect with what she loved but had strayed from—in particular, art and the creative process. She began drawing

KEEP YOUR MOURNING PERIOD SHORT

It is only human to mourn a loss, even if it is not a loved one. We mourn the loss of a promotion, the loss of a customer or trusted colleague, the loss of a job offer. It is okay to acknowledge to yourself and others that you are sad, hurt, crushed, or down in the dumps. It happens to everyone. Mourning is a natural part of healing and moving on. That said, we need to actively limit our mourning period or else it can overwhelm us.

Give yourself a deadline to pick yourself back up. Whether you feel finished mourning or not, when the date arrives, take moves to focus on the next goal and build for the next success. Sometimes taking action is the best way to get beyond our grief, but that first step can take fortitude—so commit to it on a sticky note and put it on your bathroom mirror so you can see it every morning.

and painting again and got involved with art organizations. She also reconnected with her neighboring community, establishing local rituals and relationships distinct from her professional persona. Finally, she reconnected to her sense of humor, a lifelong coping mechanism, by watching funny movies and seeking out funny people.

Over time she found herself defining who she was and how she valued herself by her daily enjoyment of life instead of by the adjectives others assigned to her. This fundamental shift helped her return to a place where she felt secure and whole.

■ ■ ■

FINALLY, SHE TOOK OWNERSHIP. Julie considered her options for returning to business leadership with a realist's eye. Even years later Pets.com loomed large anytime she spoke to anyone in the industry or the media. She also feared that ageism, rampant in high tech, would limit her options. As the Julie of today will tell you brightly, "No one would hire me because I was now old. I had *Pets* plus *old*. I knew had to figure out something to do myself."

Julie had always been the CEO of businesses others had created. Now she started looking for ideas for a business she could *found*. Not wanting to compete with Amazon, she made a list of everything that company could do better than everyone else—and everything they couldn't. With that mental map in the back of her mind, she went about the business of daily life.

Four months later she was shopping with a friend in a beautiful boutique. Her friend, who had plenty of money to spend, dragged her all the way to the back to a small consignment section. "I get Chanel, Prada, Louis Vuitton—all of it discount," her friend told her. "Who cares if someone already owned it? It looks amazing. Who's going to know? And I know the owner, so I trust these are real."

In that moment the seeds of a business took root in Julie's mind: an online consignment shop that would make the exchange frictionless for consignors and buyers alike while adding trust into the equation. Ninety days of market study, competitive differentiation, and business planning later, she received seed funding in March of 2011. Ninety more days and she had a website up. Still, she waited almost a year and $10 million in sales before going to venture capitalists to raise her Series A, convinced that her track record and the female orientation of the business would make it a hard sell without financial proof of concept. "And even then it wasn't easy," she says. As competitors popped up, she knew she was really onto something—if she could just keep up her fast pace. Five years and three rounds of funding later, she is projecting a full year of profitability in 2018—an all-too-rare phenomenon among venture-backed companies.

THE UPSIDE OF DISASTER

If perfectionism and fear of failure are looming challenges for you as they were for me, you may take comfort in learning the antidote: again, it's your network. Strong and collaborative professional relationships will carry you through almost anything. As any given professional disaster unfolds, those watching from a distance see only the negative headlines, the public shaming in black and white. But behind the scenes these are in fact peak experiences, gifts really, when convictions are tested and our true allies emerge. And if they don't feel that way as they happen, I guarantee they do with the wisdom of hindsight.

That's how Patti Hart sees it anyway, and I'm inclined to trust her. Aside from the bankruptcy at Excite@Home, Patti has sat in the hot seat many times. As Yahoo's director she took the blame for hiring short-lived CEO Scott Thompson, who had fudged the details of his bachelor's degree—a story that then led to unwarranted scrutiny of her own academic credentials. Later, while chairman of the board of International Gaming Technology, an activist investor sought to oust her. He accused her of everything from governance issues to personal use of the company jet.

She made it through all those rocky times—and even worse ones that didn't make headlines, she reminds me—by managing exactly the same way she does during periods of calm: she listened to people and made it about more than herself. "If it's about more than you on a day-to-day basis," she says. "It's about more than you when something gets hot."

Her response to a crisis always starts with honest conversations. She asks the people around her, *Do you still believe in me? Do you believe that what we're doing is the right thing? Do you believe that there's something else we should be doing?*

Says Patti, "You have to come together as a group and test your own conviction. I don't think negative things that happen like that are necessarily bad, because they cause you to inspect yourself."

Patti looks beyond her organization to tap her broader network when it comes to the practical support and information she needs during professional storms. She calls this Problem Solving 101: looking and saying, "Which resources can help me be as strong as I can be given this particular problem?" When Excite@Home went bankrupt, for example, she called upon an attorney friend who had been through it before and said, "Help me. I'm not exactly sure how to behave. I'm not sure how to make decisions differently in this situation versus in a normal operating environment. Help me."

Patti says she spends an "enormous" amount of time keeping her network well fed enough that she can pick up the phone and ask anyone she knows for ten minutes of help. But as she sees it, that investment isn't the barrier most people face when it's time to find support; what gets in their way is fear of humbling themselves enough to ask for the help. "They think they have all the answers and off they go. What they don't see is that the more you ask for help, the bigger and stronger your network becomes in that moment—and in the future too. Then you find people calling *you*."

QUIT OR STICK IT OUT?

If weathering a crisis is superglue for relationships, quitting a job in anger is dynamite. When you've been treated unfairly it can be very tempting to run, screaming or even cursing as you go. But in the end it's the opposite of "owning" your career. You're reactive, out of control, burning the bridge behind you without knowing how to cross the next chasm. You're also not doing anything to improve the situation for whomever they hire thereafter.

No major professional decision—particularly a goodbye— should ever be made on the basis of raw emotion. No matter how dire or urgent you feel the situation is, first put some distance between you and what is going on and let the adrenaline of the moment settle. You are in no shape to make a career decision if you are panicked, scared, insulted, or angry. Recently a friend told me the story of a software quality analyst she knew who had learned she was making significantly less than the other members of her team, all men. When she asked the company to bump up her pay to match, they refused, despite the fact that they were having a record year financially.

Furious, she had an angry exchange with her bosses, then decided she was going to quit. But to her credit she first confided in a group of women friends. Their unanimous feedback: "DON'T DO IT!" They urged her to stay put and file an HR complaint as well as a discrimination case with the Equal Employment Opportunity Commission. They also suggested she work on her résumé but wait to leave until she had created her next opportunity.

To all those options I might have added the suggestion to go back to her bosses, this time armed with data about the market rate for her salary as well as testimonials from colleagues about the quality of the work she did. It becomes much harder for a boss to say no when an accusation of unfairness is backed up by concrete evidence of high-quality work, thoughtfully presented.

Often it's a mistake to think that the answer to a particularly bad experience is "time off to think." Time off work should be motivated by something proactive and positive—a baby, a business idea, a passion that needs to be followed—not by a toxic experience. We get into the trap of thinking that we can't find our way to something better without first saying goodbye to the mess we're in. But I'm a big believer in staying engaged professionally and if possible, getting a regular paycheck. Burning through your savings or collecting unemployment can make even the most sangfroid among us anxious.

Lynn Perkins, for example, told me she grudgingly took a job after the failure of the startup Xuny.com, where she was a founder. Xuny.com was a forerunner to CafePress, but like Pets.com, it didn't survive the bubble burst. When cash had dwindled enough that making payroll was in jeopardy, she made the call to shut it down. "I had to tell the investors they weren't getting their money back. I had to lay everybody off," recalls Lynn. "I had built that team. I think the hardest thing for me was letting down the people who had worked for us."

When she finished shutting Xuny.com down, Lynn found herself emotionally and physically exhausted. Not knowing what to do, she opted for a midlevel analyst position at the Gap—not a passion project, but a paycheck. At the time it felt like a painful step down, going from "being a leader to being just another person on the totem pole in a large organization."

It turned out to be the best thing she could have done for herself. The stability of employment gave Lynn the time to consider what she really wanted to do with her life. She also focused on restoring herself physically, by working out more, and emotionally, by reconnecting with friends she had all but abandoned while trying to run a startup.

"It was a good recovery period. I worked there for a couple of years, and then that was it," says Lynn. "I was ready to go back on the path of doing something more interesting, and I quit."

Quitting a job is a major inflection point. Whenever possible, quit a job so you can run toward something you are excited about, not as a way to run away from something. When quitting is the only option, take the time to power UP and do what you can to normalize relationships before you walk out that door. It may not feel good in the short term, but in the long term it will serve you. If you are not given the time to normalize relationships because you are being asked to leave, circle back to your colleagues when you regain your power. You want to leave every situation and relationship confident and strong, with your head held high.

Power UP the Organization

It's never too early to start thinking about how you'll use the authority you'll inevitably earn over the course of your career to help *others* power UP. In fact, even before you have official authority, I guarantee you can find opportunities to make your corner of the new economy more inclusive and supportive not just of women but of talented people from any background, religion, race, or sexual orientation. An act as simple as suggesting your company's job postings be shared widely enough to net a diverse pool of applicants can make a difference. One of the greatest rewards of my own career was having the opportunity to chair the compensation committee at Salesforce. I took the time and care to ensure there was pay parity for both genders. There were few women outside the sales organization at the time, and sales compensation packages were very numbers driven, so it was a relatively easy undertaking. More recently, in 2016 Salesforce conducted an internal pay audit as the direct result of two senior female executives, Leyla Seka and Cindy Robbins, putting together a case and then petitioning CEO Marc Benioff directly. The eventual audit led to raises for 6 percent of employees—both men and women—with the company spending nearly $3 million to eliminate any statistically significant difference in pay. The following year, after acquiring several companies, Salesforce held another salary evaluation and raised the pay of 11 percent of employees around the world, costing an additional $3 million.

As a rule, standing up for diversity at work requires considerable contentiousness and conviction. Technology-related businesses and particularly, startups tend to move fast. Nonstop problem solving and a ticking clock predispose people to waving off higher-order priorities. Organizational efforts to increase diversity and inclusion require strong, thoughtful leadership—and I'm betting the readers of this book are just the ones to provide it.

So what is a powered-UP approach to diversifying a company? If there's an organizing principle, let it be this: *gender is not a woman's issue.* Everyone is hurt when bias leaks into hiring and the evaluation of performance. Everyone is hurt when companies select talent from a pool circumscribed by privilege rather than qualifications. Likewise, everyone is complicit in bias, not just men, although they have more positions of power so their bias does more harm. These are issues that affect all of us. As President Barack Obama wrote in *Glamour*, "The idea is that when everybody is equal, we are all more free."

Powered-UP leadership recognizes that we need to make men our partners, not our adversaries in this effort. In fact, we need them to be active leaders and speak as loudly for gender equality as women do. Like it or not, they still have most of the power, so without their leadership, progress will be glacially slow. (See the past thirty years.) Kate Mitchell, a longtime leader of the National Venture Capital Association, told me a story that epitomizes "what not to do" when it comes to this partnership. When Kate launched the association's Diversity Task Force she talked to a lot of activists, wanting to bring as many points of view to the table as possible. She recalls talking to one woman who suggested they spend money to put up a billboard on Highway 101 in San Francisco listing the name of every venture firm that didn't have a female partner. Kate's reaction: "I'm looking for actions we can take to encourage the hiring of women. Do you think shaming these men is the best way to change their behavior?"

Kate was exactly right: shaming doesn't work; it creates division and defensiveness. You know what else doesn't work? Quotas. Quotas create immediate division, invite the possibility of double standards in hiring, and create the worry that employees might be hired for reasons unrelated to their ability to do the job better than anyone else. Even the *perception* that that might be the case can be highly destructive to your team's performance and morale.

Policies and practices that protect *all of us* from bias are the single-best means for us to all power UP together.

GUARDRAILS AGAINST BIAS

Recently I got an agonized, panicked call from an entrepreneur I'm friendly with.

"Magdalena, you've got to help me," he said. "If I did something and I wasn't conscious of it, should I be blamed?"

That week, he explained, two women colleagues had sat him down in a conference room and accused him and other male leaders at his company of unconscious bias. Women weren't being treated fairly, they said, and then they rattled off a number of concrete examples to support their claim. (These women were clearly well prepared. *Brava!*) He described the meeting like dealing with two hungry lionesses backing him into a corner before eating him for lunch. He was completely intimated, a little defensive, and unsure what to do next.

After laughing with him for a moment about life in the jungle, I got serious.

"Did the women have a legitimate complaint?" I asked him. He admitted that having thought about it, he could see they did. "Then stop worrying about whether you're to blame. You're not unconscious anymore. The only question now is what you're going to do going forward."

> The most effective diversity programs are profoundly simple, action oriented, and stigmatizing to no one.

If we've learned anything over the past thirty years, it's that you can't change people overnight. Conscious and unconscious bias and outright sexism are with us and will be for a long time, maybe forever. We can police people's language, but it's a lot harder to affect what's going on in people's heads. Fortunately researchers and the companies leading the equal opportunity charge are finding out that you don't need to scrutinize people's intentions. Rather than completely remove bias from the individual, you can find ways to remove bias from the process. The most effective diversity programs are profoundly simple, action oriented, and stigmatizing to no one. They place an emphasis on simple process changes, what Dr.

TEST YOUR BIAS

Both men and women have unconscious bias. Don't believe
it? Take a free test online via Harvard's Project Implicit:
https://implicit.harvard.edu/implicit/takeatest.html.

Caroline Simard of Stanford's Clayman Institute calls "guardrails to
help people make the best possible decisions." She finds that most
people are looking to make the best decisions, to hire the best talents, without gender, race, or religious bias. But just as doctors who
know the importance of hand washing need signs reminding them
to do it, so do managers. "We find ways to remind people and provide them with what they need at the moment of decision making,"
she says.

To understand what that looks like, let's talk about the web host-
ing company GoDaddy. A few years back GoDaddy was a high-
profile icon of sexist "bro" culture, thanks to their Super Bowl
commercials, of which the raison d'être seemed to be objectifying
women. The controversy led to boycotts and fear among some inside
the company that its sexist reputation might endanger their future
IPO. In 2013 the company brought in Blake Irving as its new CEO,
and ever since, he has been working to change its reputation and
create a more diverse, inclusive culture. IPO aside, it's a wise step, as
the company is focused on serving small business owners. Although
men owned more than 70 percent of US-based small businesses in
2015, the number of women-owned businesses is growing at a much
faster clip. In short, GoDaddy needs women customers if they are to
keep growing.

Steven Aldrich, GoDaddy's chief product officer, told me that in 2015 GoDaddy employees started working with Stanford's Clayman Institute to ensure that the company was a fair and inclusive place to work. Steven and I first met because Lynn Perkins told me he was an MVP when it came to male allies. She had met him years ago through an investor and then had reconnected when they were both in the audience of a panel discussion about women in tech. He was one of the only men in the room. When Lynn asked him what brought him there, she recalls him saying, "I look around in our office, and I recognize that we have a gender problem." In particular he could see the challenges women faced in coming back to work and that, in general, it was harder for his female colleagues to get ahead. "I want to find out what I can do about it," he told Lynn, earning himself a lifetime admirer in that passing moment.

At GoDaddy, Steven tells me, Clayman Institute researchers scrutinized every touch point of an employee's experience—getting hired, getting reviewed, and getting promoted—looking for opportunities to improve the process to root out bias. The Clayman Institute also partnered with GoDaddy to embed unconscious bias training into materials to help managers and employees understand how to be fair in the workplace.

Researchers from Clayman sat in on calibration meetings, which happen twice a year. They went through the evaluation documents for those meetings and the promotion process. From there the researchers offered feedback that all focused on a single goal: eliminate ambiguity in favor of a clear set of criteria to measure employees' success.

While researching companies across the United States, Clayman's team has found that ambiguity is one of the primary channels through which unconscious bias creeps into career advancement.

When criteria aren't crystal clear, managers of both genders think they're evaluating performance when in fact they're judging employees against unconscious norms of their gender. For example, women are criticized more often than men for aggressive communication. In general Dr. Caroline Simard, the institute's research director, has found that both male and female managers hold women to a higher standard than men in their evaluations.

At GoDaddy the Clayman Institute team, working with Steven and other leaders, found that the company was doing a decent job measuring performance output, the "what" in their evaluation process. Where the company had major room to improve—like most companies—was in measuring the "how," the company's values and behaviors that employees are measured against.

Says Steven, "Our process didn't make it clear enough what values like *owns outcomes* or *joins forces* means." Leaders then worked together to create a simple set of criteria for each value, describing what great behaviors looked like, with thought toward making them gender neutral. They invited managers to bring in examples to help fuel an open discussion and further clarify the process. All the work added up to a broad redesign of the review and promotion processes and the evaluation forms that drive them.

The results, Steven told me, have been "nothing short of fantastic." Prior to the work with the Clayman Institute GoDaddy found that men were getting promoted more and seeing higher compensation increases as a result. After eighteen months of the revised process those gaps were eliminated. "I wouldn't say it happened overnight," says Steven. "But it was basically over a review cycle and a half, which was simply amazing."

Compensation gaps between men and women of similar skill sets, particularly in tech, are real and pernicious. Their effect on an individual's morale can impact the good work of an entire team. I believe women have considerable power to advocate for their own paychecks, but companies and their leadership need to share the burden of correcting this problem. Recently there's been progress as many well-known companies—among them Apple, Intel, Amazon, and Salesforce—carry out internal or third-party audits to make sure similar experience and tenure lead to similar pay.

SAY NO TO QUOTAS

Steven Aldrich from GoDaddy is outspoken in his belief that increasing diversity benefits everyone by making the business stronger. And yet we both agree that the first goal of recruitment is to find the very best candidate to do the job.

"You need to be very thoughtful about the signals you're sending to the broader organization," he says. "There's a slippery slope in telling somebody you have to hire a diverse candidate. You instantly create divisions of opinion that are not good, neither for the candidate nor for the company." In other words, you don't want people questioning whether the person who got the job deserved it.

I recently learned about an unfortunate situation in a large law firm. A couple of years back the firm realized that it was predominantly male and made a conscious decision to recruit a certain number of women associates. What made the situation unfortunate is that the recruitment criteria were not clearly defined, quantified, or standardized. Because of this ambiguity, the senior partners doubted the women recruits' qualifications, thinking that they may have been hired not solely on their merits but rather to make the target diversity hiring numbers. The senior partners then avoided bringing the women hires onto their more challenging cases, wondering whether they really had the chops to be successful. This was a terrible situation for the young women and for the senior partners. The bottom line is that everyone who gets hired needs to be held to the same clearly articulated recruitment standards.

The better route to diversity is to open up the recruitment funnel. Find a diverse pool of candidates to choose from and focus on clearly defined criteria to select the best candidate for the role. That means paying special attention to finding networks that reach women and other minorities. Already there are hiring firms such as Power to Fly and Jopwell that exist solely to help connect employers with individuals that their usual search methods don't uncover.

But here's where the practical friction arises. Managers have targets to hit and projects that need to get done. They want to fill roles as quickly as possible. So they rely mostly on their own network. And if they happen to be men—which is most often the case—their candidates are also likely be men. Very quickly they'll say, "Hey, I've got a great candidate. Let me bring him in to meet the team."

At that point it's someone like Steven Aldrich's responsibility to say, "Wait a minute. Let's open that job up, post it, and make sure people know about it internally. I'm going to ask you not to hire for that role until you've seen at least one qualified female candidate. You don't have to hire her, but you need to take the time to find her."

One organization that has been very creative in opening the recruitment funnel to more women is Etsy, the online marketplace for handmade goods. Etsy leaders wanted to hire more female engineers, but they were finding that the junior candidates who came their way typically didn't have enough hands-on experience. Their solution was to establish Hacker School, a three-month, full-time program with the explicit aim of preparing students, both men and women, for employment at Etsy. After running just two sessions in 2012

Etsy had expanded the number of female engineers at the company by 18 percent, as First Round Capital, one of Etsy's investors, proudly shared on its website. The percentage of female engineers at Etsy has since grown even more dramatically.

As for keeping bias out of the selection process itself, Stanford's Dr. Simard offers a simple recommendation. Anyone reviewing résumés should sit with a checklist of the top three criteria for the position, comparing each résumé against the list. This laser focus on specific requirements is better than working from the job description—again, it eliminates ambiguity.

When Simard works directly with companies, she makes sure that managers are part of the conversation from the get-go. "Really engaging them in the co-creation of these solutions is fundamental so that it doesn't feel like something that's coming from HR or from the Clayman Institute or something outside," she says. Together they create simple yet effective tools such as checklists, not onerous guidelines that make the hiring managers' jobs more difficult.

TAKE YOUR VALUES TO WORK

As a leader, you'll be the one with the responsibility for defining and articulating the values that an organization holds dear. Businesses can't power UP without employees who care about the work they're doing and the impact it has on other employees and beyond.

It's also appropriate—in fact, necessary—for you to turn to your own values system to help you make decisions. This is true at any point in your career. We are humans, and the more we embrace our full humanity at work, the more we can avoid the ethical tragedies that have recently made headlines at many of our financial institutions and yes, at some tech companies.

THE BUSINESS CASE FOR DIVERSITY

There is strong research showing that having more women, particularly as senior leaders, leads to improved performance. Here's a summary of the most widely shared stats to have at your fingertips as you advocate for change[1]:

- A gender-diverse workforce outperforms revenue earnings of a gender-homogenous workforce by 41 percent.

- Offices where the employees think the firm is accepting of diversity tend to be more cooperative.

- Companies with more women senior managers outperform companies with proportionally fewer women at the top. Women CEOs in the Fortune 1000 drive three times the returns as S&P 500 enterprises run predominantly by men.

- Women-led high-tech startups generate higher revenues per dollar of invested capital and have lower failure rates than those led by men.

- Public companies with more women on the board have significantly better short- and long-term financial performance.

If you hold a position of power, you have a great opportunity to bring your personal values into the corporate culture—which certainly will include a passionate commitment to equal opportunity for all and true meritocracy. But it doesn't stop there. It meant a great deal to me that I could play a significant role in the first six years of Salesforce's life, having a hand in setting strategy and interacting directly with the employees.

DEFINE YOUR MISSION

Give some thought to your personal values and vision, then write them down and post them somewhere in your work space. On a regular basis ask yourself

▌ Does my company share my values? If not, what can I do?

▌ Are my actions in line with my values?

▌ Am I articulating my values to my colleagues and employees?

Values help companies and teams sail through turbulent waters. After Salesforce went public and our stock value was oscillating up and down, Marc Benioff asked me to address all the employees in an all-hands meeting. In my talk I urged them not to pay much attention to the fluctuations, which could be emotionally draining. Instead, I wanted them to judge their success by how well they were serving our long-term vision and values. Being a sailor, I used a related analogy to make my point: the easiest way to avoid getting seasick in turbulent waters is to keep one's eye on the destination or out toward the horizon if no land is in sight. Just last year during Salesforce's annual Dreamforce conference a middle-aged man pulled me aside and said, "I remember your talk years back. I still have my eye on the destination—and I still have my original stock!" Values stay with people, guiding them even as immediate business priorities change.

One of my most vivid Salesforce memories had nothing to do with any business milestone. About three years into Salesforce's life, we had set up a board call to discuss an urgent matter. I was on the phone with another board member, and we were waiting on the line for Marc to join us. We chatted for a few minutes, and then a few minutes more. Still no Marc. To understand the dynamic, you need to remember that this wasn't the celebrity-CEO Marc Benioff of today; we were still a small company, and boards have the power to hire and fire CEOs. Although our relationship with Marc certainly wasn't hierarchical, this was a guy making his bosses wait.

I emailed Marc, asking him where he was. He immediately replied, "On another call, will be with you shortly. Mahalo." I was annoyed. I'm a big believer in punctuality and respecting your colleagues' time.

Finally Marc joined us. "Please tell me you were late because you were closing a multiyear deal with a huge prospect," I blasted.

Marc's reply took me completely by surprise.

"I was on the phone with my grandmother," he said with a smile in his voice but an apologetic tone. Alone in my office, I must've done a double take. I found myself go from irritation to a broad smile in a heartbeat.

"Magdalena, if it were anyone else, I would have never made you guys wait. But it was my grandmother. I just couldn't hang up on her." I couldn't argue with that! I finally responded, "Marc, all I can say is that I hope someday to have a grandchild with your values of love, care, and respect for the family's elders."

I'm sure we went on to have a highly productive call, though I have no idea what that "urgent issue" was. But for the rest of my life I will always remember Marc Benioff's strong personal values and how he was not afraid to bring them to his company.

Your values and integrity, expressed in both words and action, will be remembered when all the other details of your contributions are long forgotten. They are your legacy. But more importantly, they are your greatest source of power to bring positive change, both for yourself and all those around you.

My hope is that the face of technology tomorrow isn't just more female or more diverse but that it's even more committed to promoting values that empower everyone. The products and services you build have the potential to change the world for the better—or not. Whether you're a founder, an employee, a middle manager, or an activist, your choices will determine the shape of future industries. That's what makes the new economy so inspiring to so many. Take that responsibility seriously, and recognize it as a rare opportunity: it is a chance to power UP so much more than just yourself.

Epilogue: Starting from Scratch

These days when my phone rings, it's often not CEO Marc Benioff or fellow mom Meg Whitman on the line or anyone else from my Silicon Valley network. It's a single mom from Fresno, California, or someone like her. She needs a car to get to work, but she does not know if she can get a car loan, and if she did, how much it would cost her per month. She is worried because she went into bankruptcy over an $800 medical debt. Can I guide her to a lender for an auto loan?

We are talking because I'm the cofounder of a new consumer finance startup called DriveInformed. Our mission is to increase access and to provide a better car loan experience for people buying used cars. I'm tackling a new industry I know little about, and talking to customers is the best way to learn the market and understand their needs. I literally wrote the book on how to succeed in the new economy, and here I am again, answering customer calls and feeling like a total novice. I don't know how our company will change over the course of the next few years, what challenges we will face, what rewards we will celebrate. Once again I am starting, in many ways, from scratch.

This is the future of anyone who embarks on the exciting adventure of a career in technology. I started my career in semiconductors, moved into computer systems, later into software, online services, Internet access, electronic payments, electronic commerce infrastructure, and on it goes. You pick up some wisdom along the way, but the learning, the fumbling, and the humbling never ends. The ones who do well are the ones who don't just embrace but celebrate this truth. You can't just live it; you've got to love it.

And yet my learnings this go-round are hitting me more deeply than ever before. Our startup's market is the millions of folks who need car loans, including those who have credit histories that banks today won't touch. These are the so-called subprimes, a demeaning label now associated with the world's most historic banking fiasco, but it happens to apply to the credit histories of more than half of our American population. When that woman from Fresno calls, I use DriveInformed's technology and available data to show auto lenders that despite her past bankruptcy, she can now afford to pay her car loan. It's a practical challenge with a heavy emotional reality: I'm working to find a solution that will keep this woman from having her life ruined over an $800 road bump in her recent past.

We talk a lot about the echo chamber in Silicon Valley: when everyone you're talking to is just like you, all you hear is your own voice, your own thinking repeated back to you. I've never felt this so strongly as I have recently after spending time on the phone with so many strangers from so many different parts of the United States, parts I have never stepped foot in.

For the first time ever the core of my business is focused on powering UP people who aren't in a moment when they can think about powering UP themselves. Most are living paycheck to paycheck, focused entirely on survival. The experience has personally been highly transformative. For me and for everyone in the company, from our engineers to our investors, the mission is clear and central to every decision. I have always worked with conviction in the importance of my work, no matter the company. But seeing the huge potential impact of our product and technology on the daily lives of millions of Americans gives me a passion beyond what I've known before.

This experience compels me to leave you with one final parting message: never be content with operating inside the bubble that naturally forms around each of us if we let it. Fight each and every day to discover new ways to find and connect with people who don't look like you, think like you, or know the things you know. Doing this takes an effort, whether your network is Silicon Valley investors, Ivy Leaguers, community college grads, or the kids from the very neighborhood where you grew up and still live.

Any enclosed circle will limit your potential as a businessperson and entrepreneur. If you understand only the few, you'll never operate a business that scales to serve the many. And if the future of the new economy is taking technology and applying it to new areas and traditional industries, much of the opportunity lies outside of the worlds that our top universities expose us to. Those of us operating from a position of privilege need to get out of our own backyards so we can understand the broader customer base, not just the early adopters.

But more importantly, whatever your starting place, getting outside of your bubble is the best way to broaden yourself and your aspirations as a human being. I've never felt a stronger call to serve customers than I do today, having spent these past months with an up close view of so many people's life struggles. What makes it especially amazing is that I have my firstborn son, Justin Wickett, to thank: DriveInformed is his brainchild. Talk about coming full circle in parenthood—your children making you a better entrepreneur! And my second son, Troy Wickett, advises us regularly on the complexity of the financial services industry. As we've hired engineers at DriveInformed, I am so happy to see that young people today are interested in evaluating the mission of companies before they join and are willing to forgo fatter salaries from companies they do not see as mission driven for companies that match their values.

Getting out of your echo chamber and living your values every day doesn't require you to devote yourself to social entrepreneurship, of course. Reaching out to others can take many forms. It can happen through travel or volunteer work. For those in a position to hire, it can happen by taking steps to make sure your applicants come from all walks of life by focusing on "culture add" not just "culture fit," as a recent *New York Times* article so deftly put it. It can even happen by watching a documentary or reading a book about a problem or place that's foreign to you or expanding your digital network beyond its natural limits. But ultimately I urge you to connect with new people and places face-to-face. Put yourself out there—literally.

The more we as women hold close the mission of powering others UP along with ourselves, the more groundbreaking our efforts will be and the more profound their impact. I truly believe that's the future of good business and capitalism. Customers today expect companies to have values beyond their most recent PR campaign, and they're voting with their wallets.

But hold close one caveat: even in a life committed to doing good for others, there are moments when you should be selfish—when you must be selfish. As women, and particularly for those of us who become mothers, our default can become to take care of others first. It's a fine impulse, one I believe is a powerful driver of success. But it's up to you to find the balance so you're not shortchanging yourself in the process.

We may not be able to control our surroundings, the market's reaction to our product, our customer's budget, our competitor's moves, our boss's point of view, our team's behavior, or our spouses, partners, children, and even what happens to our own bodies. Every life and every career will have challenges and moments of pure devastation. It's never more important than in those moments to keep our heads and our spirits high by living and acting with integrity and belief in who we are. That's the ultimate guide for our relationship not only with others but also with ourselves. Powering UP is always an option, and I promise you that it beats the alternative.

So now as we leave each other, I throw a symbolic bucket of water behind you, just as my parents and neighbors did when I left to start my life in America. And I leave you with this wish:

May you flow, sometimes roaring and sometimes calm, but always moving forward toward the sea you yearn to reach.

ACKNOWLEDGMENTS

Neither my life nor my career would be possible without the selfless love and infinite support of my mother Selma Yeşil. Thank you, Mom, for always being there. I owe my life to you. And to my father, Kevork Yeşil, you are the original author of *Power UP*. In this book, I attempted to share your teachings, which have served me so well, especially in your absence. Thank you for teaching me how to Power UP at a very young age and for giving me the luxury to do so at a place and time when little girls were not allowed such behavior. I am also grateful for the adventurous spirit and the gift of independence you instilled in me; they have enabled me to take risks throughout my career.

I owe a big thank you to those who have helped me Power UP throughout my life:

My classmates of UAKL76 and my friends in Kinali and Moda, for your friendship, support, and for making your home mine after I no longer had my own home in Turkey.

All my employers and bosses, for giving me the privilege to work, for helping me transform into a businessperson, and for showcasing my successes without reservations.

All my teams at my various operating companies and the management teams of my portfolio companies; I would not have the career I enjoy without your cooperation, hard work, and dedication. You made going to work every day an adventure and solving difficult problems a fun challenge. I am honored to be associated with each of you.

I have had amazing role models and sponsors in my career to learn from and try to emulate. Dan Lynch, my cofounder in two startups, you showed me how to keep my spirits bright even in the darkest days of start-up gloom and doom; Eric Schmidt, for your partnership and your support throughout my days of entrepreneurship; Irwin Federman, my partner at USVP, for your pearls of wisdom on life and early stage investing; Sandy Robertson, for modeling true board leadership at Salesforce and RPX; Craig Ramsey, for being my partner on the Salesforce compensation committee and at DriveInformed; Garry Mathiason, for your guidance through the complexities of organizational behavior. I am very lucky to have each one of you as a source of aspiration.

Marc Benioff, for placing your trust and confidence in me as we built Salesforce and for giving the Company your all and then some. You have been an incredible leader, not just for Salesforce and the cloud movement but also for gender equality. And a huge thank you for your awesome foreword to *Power UP*.

Parker Harris, for always being a pleasure to work with, starting from our first phone call; watching you evolve over these past years has been humbling. Frank Dominguez, Dave Moellenhoff, Jim Cavalieri, Jim Steele, Courtney Broadus, Steve Garnett, Jim Steele, Dave Orrico, Nancy Connery, Frank van Veenendaal, Steve Cakebread, Tien Tzou, Paul Nakada, and Caryn Marooney for your devotion and hard work.

The visionary Sonja Perkins and Jennifer Fonstad, my co-founders at Broadway Angels, for helping countless women Power UP. I am one of them.

My team at DriveInformed for your amazing energy and dedication to our mission.

Steve Manion, Georgine Muntz, Stephanie Alsbrooks, and Bill Nemecek for helping me power UP in a brand new industry.

I am indebted to all of the incredible leaders who so generously shared their personal stories, career learnings and advice: Steve Aldrich, Ruzwana Bashir, Gina Bianchini, Courtney Broadus, Leah Busque, Lara Druyan, Jennifer Fonstad, Theresia Gouw, Patti Hart, Julia Hartz, Debby Hopkins, Jennifer Hyman, Lynn Jurich, Lynne Laube, Kate Mitchell, Claudia Fan Munce, Tanja Omeze, Lynn Perkins, Sonja Perkins, Meaghan Rose, Debra Rossi, Clara Shih, Caroline Simard, Debbie Sterling, Julie Wainwright, Heidi Zak, Michelle Zatlyn, Lucy Zhang. You enriched Power UP beyond my experiences, making it a truly powerful tool for success in the new economy. I cherish having you in my book and in my life.

Many have given me the encouragement to write this book by motivating me, reading portions of the manuscript, and sharing their opinions. Carlye Adler, who told me I had this book in me long before I knew it myself, and who encouraged me every step of the way; Steve Blank, who made it clear that I owed Power UP to the next generation, because if we do not teach them what we have learned through our experiences, who will; Betsy Blumenthal, for helping me find my voice in the early days of writing; Mik Flynn for powering me UP not just inside but also outside with her amazing fashion taste; Beth Gordon, Karen King, Katie Kulik, Nichole Mustard, and Laura Stein, each one of you contributed in your unique way.

Power UP would not have become the book you are reading if it were not for my incredible team of supporters and collaborators.

Sara Grace, my amazing writing partner, who agreed to collaborate with me, knowing English was my fourth language. I thank you for your dedication to the mission. Your magic with the written word and your ability to distill messages was fantastic to watch. I loved our times together.

Karen Murphy, you made this project possible by introducing me to the best professionals in the business, each with extraordinary talent. I owe the *Power UP* dream team to you. I also appreciated your invaluable feedback on my blind spots.

Dan Farber, thank you for keeping me away from the other formats I was contemplating and for encouraging me to share my personal stories in my own voice.

Jim Levine, my wonderful agent and guide into the world of publishing. Thank you for always being there with your wise advice when I need you.

Laura Mazer, my editor, whose early notes contributed so much to the book's structure, clarity, and style, and without whom we might have never discovered and articulated the book's defining mantra. Thank you to *Power UP*'s very able editorial producer Lori Hobkirk from the Book Factory and her entire production crew; our lovely copy editor Josephine Mariea; tireless publicist Sharon Kunz; and Kevin Hanover, Mathew Weston, and Quinn Fariel on the marketing team at Hachette, who dug in to make *Power UP* a success.

Nicolas Saad, for bringing your artistic, technical and editorial talents to creating and managing *Power UP*'s online home at www.magdalena.com and at www.powerupguide.com.

My family, who has been by my side me throughout my career while enduring me as wife or mother- Jim, for your unconditional support of whatever professional endeavor I chose to pursue over the years and for being my sounding board; Justin for collaborating with me on numerous ventures, bringing me back to entrepreneurship after a decade and teaching me that the consumer we serve is our most important customer; Troy, for your sage business advice and insights beyond your years. I also thank you for spending your limited days of Christmas break reading, editing, and giving me detailed feedback on my manuscript, and re-reading tirelessly.

Lastly, I want to thank this amazing country we call America and her people, for welcoming me as an immigrant with open arms when I had nothing to offer in return, giving me a great education followed by the opportunity to put that education to work, and finally for creating an environment for a woman like me to thrive and make a meaningful contribution. Above all, for valuing human rights and freedoms, and for being a place to live without fear.

I am very blessed and much obliged,

Magdelena

THE EXECUTIVES OF POWER UP

▌ STEVEN ALDRICH

As chief product officer at GoDaddy, Steven Aldrich sets and executes the company's vision of providing elegant, end-to-end technology solutions for more than 14 million small business customers. Steven brings more than a decade of experience at Intuit, where he built solutions to help small businesses use the web to grow and run their stores. He also has small-business experience as the founder of an online company that simplified shopping for insurance. Steven earned a master's degree in business from Stanford and a bachelor's degree in physics from the University of North Carolina. After hours, he serves as board president of the Bay Area Glass Institute—a nonprofit glass studio—and enjoys spending time with his wife, Allison, and their son, Jackson, at many sports and arts events.

▌ RUZWANA BASHIR

Ruzwana Bashir cofounded Peek Travel, Inc. and also serves as its CEO. Ms. Bashir is a travel junkie, having navigated her way through forty countries. She previously worked at Gilt Groupe, Art.sy, the Blackstone Group, and Goldman Sachs. She was president of the Oxford Union at Oxford University. She has an MBA from Harvard Business School, where she was a Fulbright Scholar, and a BA in economics from Oxford University.

▌ GINA BIANCHINI

Gina Bianchini is the founder and chief executive officer of Mighty Networks, the most powerful, effective organizing platform for interest-based social networks on mobile available today. It's home to fifty thousand interest networks and growing.

Before Mighty Networks Bianchini and Marc Andreessen co-founded Ning, a pioneering social platform for niche networks online. Under her leadership Ning grew to 90 million people across 3 million social networks and three hundred thousand active communities in entertainment, politics, education, and culture. She started her career at Goldman Sachs as a financial analyst in the high technology group.

Gina also serves on the board of directors of Scripps Networks (SNI), which owns HGTV, the Food Network, and the Travel Channel, and also cofounded LeanIn.Org, an organization dedicated to supporting women leaning into their ambitions. She grew up in Cupertino, California, graduated with honors from Stanford University, and received her MBA from Stanford Business School.

▌ COURTNEY BROADUS

Courtney Broadus is an adviser and consulting technology executive to startups and cloud computing companies. She has held executive leadership and management positions in technology for over fifteen years at both startups and Fortune 500 companies, most recently as a technology SVP at Salesforce.com, where she worked for ten years. Under her leadership the team grew from two to over three hundred and defined the industry standard for consistently delivering scalable, reliable cloud computing applications with renowned quality that customers love. Prior to Salesforce.com Courtney held technology leadership positions at Oracle and engineering/architect roles at several startups. Courtney is passionate about helping startups execute, deliver, scale, and build excellent teams founded on strong cultures.

▌ LEAH BUSQUE

Leah Busque has fifteen years experience building and creating technology products that have reached millions of people around the globe. She started her career at IBM as a software engineer in the software group, working on Lotus Notes and Domino. In 2008 Leah founded TaskRabbit, the leading on-demand service marketplace in the world. She served as the CEO for eight years and now is the executive chairwoman of the company. In 2014 Leah was inaugurated into the Forum of Young Global Leaders, a prestigious group of fewer than one thousand people around the globe recognized for their bold, brave, action-oriented entrepreneurial ventures. The arts and creating opportunities for women in technology are important to her, and she also serves on the board of the Silicon Valley Ballet.

Leah resides in the Bay Area of California with her husband, two children, and highly energetic black Labrador retriever. She graduated magna cum laude from Sweet Briar College, where she earned a BS in mathematics and computer science.

▌ LARA DRUYAN

Lara Druyan is a managing director at the Royal Bank of Canada, where she is the head of Innovation on the West Coast. She is responsible for identifying and working with startups on the bank's behalf, creating partnerships, establishing relationships with the Silicon Valley ecosystem and new product creation, and investing in startups that are strategic to the bank. Previously she was the founding partner of G&B Partners, an investment and advisory firm focused on technology companies. She also served as a venture partner for Almaz Capital, an adviser to Pilot Growth Equity, and as a venture adviser to SRI, where she helped them conceive of, launch, and incubate new ventures. Ms. Druyan served as vice chair of the board of trustees and chair of the investment committee for the City of San Jose's Federated Employee Retirement System (a $2 billion pension plan) for six years. Previously she was an investor in residence at U.S. Venture Partners and a general partner for over a decade with early-stage venture capital firm Allegis Capital. Lara also worked at Silicon Graphics as a product manager in its heyday and released a dozen software products while at SGI. In 2016 she was named as one of the Silicon Valley Investors You Need to Know by *Inc.*

▌ JENNIFER FONSTAD

Jennifer Fonstad is a cofounder of Aspect Ventures, an early-stage, mobile-focused investment firm with $150 million under management. Prior to Aspect Jennifer was a managing director with Draper Fisher Jurvetson for almost two decades as a part of the team that grew that firm from $150 million under management to over $3.5 billion before she left to found Aspect. While at DFJ Jennifer led the formation of and sat on the investment committees of several DFJ affiliate funds, including DFJ Vietnam and DFJ Israel, as well as serving as an adviser to DFJ China.

Jennifer's success as an investor has landed her on the *Forbes* Midas List twice as well as an AO Power Player 2012 and 2013. In 2016 she was named Deloitte Venture Capitalist of the Year. Jennifer graduated cum laude from Georgetown University and holds an MBA with distinction from the Harvard Business School. Before joining Bain & Company she spent a year teaching math to high school students in sub-Saharan Africa. She spends weekends running around with her four children.

▎ THERESIA GOUW

Theresia Gouw is an engineer, experienced entrepreneur, and successful investor in the new mobility space, focused primarily on security, data analytics, and consumer opportunities.

She recently cofounded Aspect Ventures, where she led the firm's early investments in Cato Networks, Exabeam, ForeScout, the Muse, SelfScore, BirchBox, and BaubleBar. Prior to Aspect Theresia was a partner at Accel, where she championed many successful companies through IPOs or acquisitions, including Imperva (IMPV), Trulia (TRLA), LearnVest (Northwestern Mutual), Jasper Design (CDNS), and Kosmix (WMT).

As an entrepreneur Theresia was founding vice president of business development and sales at Release Software, a venture-backed company that provided SaaS to enable digital rights management and payment technologies for the software industry. Earlier she worked at Bain & Company and as a product manager at Silicon Graphics. Theresia holds a ScB in engineering from Brown University, magna cum laude, and an MBA from Stanford University.

▎ PATTI S. HART

As chief executive officer of International Game Technology (IGT) from 2009 to 2015, Patti S. Hart led one of the most innovative and profitable gaming companies in the world. Ms. Hart has served on IGT's board of directors since June 2006. Following the 2015 sale of IGT to Gtech, Ms. Hart assumed the role of vice chairman of the board.

Prior to joining IGT she was the chairman and CEO of Pinnacle Systems, Inc. from 2004 to 2005 and of Excite@Home, Inc. from 2001 to 2002. Ms. Hart was previously chairman and CEO of Telocity, Inc. and held various executive positions at the Sprint Corporation from 1986 to 1999. Hart has served shareholders through her numerous appointments to public company boards of directors. In addition to IGT, she has served on many boards, including Plantronics Corporation, Korn Ferry, Yahoo, Spansion, Pharmaceutical Product Development (PPD, Inc.), Vantive, Premisys, Excite@Home, Telocity, and Pinnacle Systems.

She holds a bachelor's degree in business administration with an emphasis in marketing and economics from Illinois State University.

▌ JULIA HARTZ

Julia Hartz is an entrepreneur, investor, and the cofounder and CEO of Eventbrite, which powers more than 2 million events around the world each year. Under her leadership the company has generated billions in gross ticket sales, processes more than 2 million tickets per week to events and experiences in 180 countries, and is consistently recognized for their award-winning culture and workplace. Julia has been honored as one of *Fortune*'s 2015 40 Under 40 business leaders, *Inc.*'s 35 under 35 in 2014, and *Fortune*'s Most Powerful Women Entrepreneurs in 2013, and she has been profiled for her leadership and impact in top publications around the world. Julia landed in Silicon Valley via Hollywood, where she began her career as a development executive at MTV and FX Networks.

▌ DEBORAH HOPKINS

Deborah Hopkins is Citi's chief innovation officer and CEO of Citi Ventures. Ms. Hopkins founded and built Citi Ventures recognizing the critical role innovation must play in driving growth at Citi amid accelerating disruptive forces and heightened customer expectations. A lifelong change agent, Ms. Hopkins partners with Citi's businesses to shepherd creativity and implement breakthrough solutions. Based in Palo Alto, her team works to connect Citi to the Silicon Valley entrepreneurial ecosystem through their work in venture investing, identification of transformative trends, sponsorship of a network of labs and accelerators across the company, and bringing the adoption of Lean Start Up to the enterprise.

Since joining Citi in 2003 Ms. Hopkins has served in a number of executive roles, including head of corporate strategy as well as mergers and acquisitions and chief operations and technology officer. She continues to act as a senior adviser to Citi's Global Investment Bank. Her experience prior to Citi spans multiple industries—automotive, aerospace, telecommunications and information technology. Previous roles include chief financial officer at both Boeing and Lucent Technologies, vice president of finance at General Motors Europe, and general auditor at General Motors.

▌ JENNIFER HYMAN

Jennifer Hyman is the cofounder and CEO of Rent the Runway, a fashion company with a technology soul that is disrupting the way women get dressed. In her role she sets the strategic priorities of the business and leads the company in growing all areas of the business, including marketing, technology, product, and analytics. She cofounded Rent the

Runway in 2009 with Jennifer Fleiss and has since raised over $190 million in venture capital, growing the business to over 6 million members, eleven hundred employees, and 450 designer brands. Jennifer has been honored with numerous recognitions, including Tribeca Film Festival's Disruptive Innovation Awards; *Fortune's* Trailblazers: 11 People Changing Business in 2013, Most Powerful Women Entrepreneurs, and 40 Under 40; *Inc.'s* 30 Under 30; and *Fast Company's* Most Influential Women in Technology.

▌ LYNN JURICH

Lynn Jurich is chief executive officer and cofounder of Sunrun (RUN), the largest dedicated residential solar company in the United States. With Sunrun cofounder Ed Fenster Lynn invented the business model "solar as a service" that unlocked consumer demand for clean, affordable energy direct from residential rooftops. Today, with more than $3 billion in installed solar systems across fifteen states, Sunrun is revolutionizing how consumers get electricity. Before Sunrun Lynn worked at Summit Partners where, as one of few female venture capitalists, she completed investments with an aggregate market value of over $900 million in the financial services and technology sectors. Lynn was named *Fast Company's* Most Creative People in Business in 2013 and *Forbes's* Women to Watch in 2015. Lynn earned her BS in science, technology, and society, and MBA from Stanford University. In her free time Lynn brings her competitive spirit to the tennis court and nurtures her appreciation of nature with long walks. As a new mom, she also loves spending time with her daughter and husband.

▎ LYNNE LAUBE

Lynne Laube, the founder and CEO of Cardyltics, is an accomplished executive who has been leading step change innovation for over twenty years. In 2008 she founded Cardlytics, an analytics platform that makes marketing more relevant and measurable. Cardlytics uses its proprietary analytics to help advertisers better target customers and "close the loop" using actual purchases to measure marketing effectiveness. In 2016 Cardlytics was named one of the fastest growing companies in America by Deloitte Fast 500 and *Inc.* 5000.

Before founding Cardlytics Lynne held multiple executive positions with Capital One and played a key role in the formation and growth of the US credit card business and expansion and in the UK as well as several new US business lines including small business, cobrand partnerships, and payments. Lynne holds a BS in finance and marketing from University of Cincinnati's College of Business and is a graduate of Darden's Executive Leadership program at UVA.

▎ KATE MITCHELL

Kate is a cofounder of Scale Venture Partners, which invests in early-in-revenue technology companies. She and the ScaleVP team have backed successful high-growth companies including Box, Docusign, ExactTarget (SalesForce), Omniture (Adobe), and RingCentral. Kate is past chairman and current board member of the National Venture Capital Association (NVCA) and remains active in policy matters that impact startups and innovation. She coauthored the IPO section of the 2012 JOBS Act and currently cochairs the NVCA Inclusion & Diversity Task Force, which focuses on advancing opportunities for women and minorities across the venture ecosystem. Mitchell received the NVCA Outstanding Service Award in 2013 for her policy work on behalf of the venture industry. She serves on the board of SVB Financial Group (SIVB), Fortive Corporation (FTV), and the Silicon Valley Community Foundation. Kate is also a member of the NASDAQ Private Market Advisory Board and a commentator on technology trends for CNBC *Squawk Alley.*

▌ CLAUDIA FAN MUNCE

Claudia Fan Munce joined New Enterprise Associates in 2016 after thirty years of service with IBM, where she held many technical and business leadership positions. She founded the Venture Capital Group within IBM, where she served as its managing director and vice president of corporate development. The Venture Capital Group is a unit in IBM that drives nonorganic growth through partnerships and M&A activities globally, focusing on growth markets and disruptive technology and business models. Prior to that position she headed the licensing and commercialization group in the IBM Research Lab.

Claudia is frequently cited as a pioneer and leader in the corporate venture community and contributed to many articles on corporate venture innovation published in *Business Week*, the *Wall Street Journal*, the *New York Times*, and others. In the March 2015 issue of the *Worth* magazine she was named one of the twenty most powerful players in Silicon Valley.

Claudia was born in Taiwan and grew up in Brazil. She holds a master's degree in computer science from Santa Clara University School of Engineering and a master's degree in management from Stanford University Graduate School of Business.

▌ TANJA OMEZE

Tanja Omeze is the head of marketing for the Amazon Video Store. She has more than fifteen years experience in digital and traditional marketing, e-commerce, and mobile tech, with more than ten years leading teams at both early-stage and F500 companies. She is the former head of marketing and analytics for Verizon Wireless, where she launched the Smart Home showcase and AppFinder. She has deep expertise in IoT, apps, tech, mobile, retail, education, health, financial services, and publishing, and she has worked for and with many leading brands.

▌ LYNN PERKINS

Lynn Perkins is CEO and cofounder of *UrbanSitter*, a mobile and online service that is reinventing the way parents find trusted childcare. After launching in 2011, Lynn quickly grew UrbanSitter into a national marketplace in less than a year. To date, more than 2 million hours of babysitting have occurred on the platform across sixty cities.

An Internet startup veteran, Lynn's work with UrbanSitter is her third startup experience. Previously she served as founder and CEO of Xuny.com and vice president of business development at Bridgepath .com. She also held roles focused on real estate strategy, services, and transactions for Joie de Vivre Hospitality, the Gap, and LaSalle Partners.

A successful "mompreneur," Lynn relies on many things to keep her energized, including a daily 6:30 a.m. wake-up from her three kids, a good cappuccino, working with a great team, solving real-world problems, and of course, great babysitters!

▌ SONJA PERKINS

Sonja Hoel Perkins is considered one of the best-performing and most senior women in venture capital. Investing broadly in all stages and areas of information technology throughout her career, she has been able to move successfully with the times—from the PC to networking to the Internet to mobile and consumer. Her career "home runs"—where she was the start-up investor—include AcmePacket (APKT), F5 Networks (FFIV), McAfee Associates (acquired by Intel), and Q1 Labs (acquired by IBM). Several of Sonja's companies have achieved multibillion-dollar valuations. In 2015, *Worth* magazine ranked Sonja #98 among the 100 Most Powerful People in Finance in the World.

Sonja focuses also on her family and community. She is the founder of Project Glimmer, a non-profit organization that inspires at-risk teenage girls and women to believe in themselves by letting them know their community cares.

▌ MEAGHAN ROSE

Meaghan Rose is founder and CEO of Rocksbox.com, a technology-driven jewelry retail company. Prior to starting Rocksbox, Meaghan was with McKinsey & Co., where she led product innovation and retail strategy for consumer packaged goods, beauty, and technology clients across the United States and Asia. It was in this role that Meaghan began to realize that the traditional retail experience was simply not built to serve today's woman. Meaghan started Rocksbox with the mission to serve and inspire women—and the aspiration to create a jewelry retail experience that allowed women to discover and experiment with jewelry without the commitment of buying.

Meaghan learned to code and launched Rocksbox beta from her living room and with her own jewelry collection. Today Rocksbox serves women across the country, supported by a distribution team in Ohio and an HQ team in San Francisco.

▌ DEBRA ROSSI

Formerly, Debra Rossi was the executive vice president at Wells Fargo and CEO and member of the board of directors of Wells Fargo Merchant Services, LLC. Rossi was responsible for the overall business strategy and management of Wells Fargo Merchant Services, which provided payment services for retail and corporate customers and processed nearly $300 billion in payments annually. Under her leadership Wells Fargo Merchant Services has generated double-digit growth in sales volume for the past five years.

A twenty-nine-year veteran of Wells Fargo, Rossi has held multiple leadership roles across the company, including Merchant Services, Business Internet Services, and eCommerce Payments. She was responsible for leading many of the payment innovations that are commonplace today. Under her guidance Wells Fargo launched the first US point-of-sale debit and credit solution for a grocery store in 1988 and for a quick-service restaurant in 1989. In 1995 Rossi led Wells Fargo in becoming the first bank to process a secure credit card transaction on the Internet.

In 2001 she was named one of the year's Most Influential Executives by *Future Banker* magazine. In 2011 Rossi was the first woman to receive the Electronic Transactions Association's highest honor, the Distinguished Payments Professional Award.

▌ CLARA SHIH

Clara Shih is CEO and founder of Hearsay, whose predictive analytics technology helps salespeople reach out to clients at the right time with the right message while staying in compliance with industry regulations. A pioneer in the social media industry, Clara developed the first social business application in 2007 and subsequently authored the *New York Times*–featured best seller, *The Facebook Era*. Her latest book, *The Social Business Imperative: Adapting Your Business Model to the Always-Connected Customer*, was released in April 2016.

Clara has been named one of *Fortune's* Most Powerful Women Entrepreneurs, *Fast Company's* Most Influential People in Technology, *BusinessWeek's* Top Young Entrepreneurs, and both *Fortune's* and *Ad Age's* 40 Under 40. She is a member of the Starbucks board of directors and previously served in a variety of technical, product, and marketing roles at Google, Microsoft, and Salesforce.com.

▌CAROLINE SIMARD

Caroline Simard is passionate about building better workplaces for women through evidence-based solutions. As research director for Stanford's Clayman Institute for Gender Research, she is responsible for leading research designed to build more effective and inclusive organizations. Previously she was associate director of diversity and leadership at the Stanford School of Medicine, where she implemented innovative models for increasing work-life integration to increase faculty satisfaction and retention.

Prior to joining Stanford University Caroline was vice president of research and executive programs at the Anita Borg Institute (ABI) for Women and Technology, where she led the creation and dissemination of research-based solutions to increase gender diversity in scientific and technical careers, working with leading technology companies and academic institutions. She drove ABI's first collaborative research project with the Clayman Institute, Climbing the Technical Ladder, receiving global media attention. She founded and designed the first industry benchmarking initiative for women in technical roles across levels and created executive programs designed to accelerate change in companies.

▮ DEBBIE STERLING

Debbie is the founder and CEO of GoldieBlox. Her award-winning children's multimedia company is disrupting the pink aisle in toy stores globally and challenging gender stereotypes with the world's first girl engineer character. Debbie is an engineer, entrepreneur, and one of the leaders in the movement to get girls interested in STEM (science, technology, engineering, and math). Debbie was named *TIME*'s Person of the Moment, honored by the National Retail Foundation as one of twenty-five People Shaping Retail's Future, and was recently added to *Fortune*'s prestigious 40 Under 40 list. In 2015 Debbie was inducted as a Presidential Ambassador for Global Entrepreneurship and honored by the National Women's History Museum with a Living Legacy Award for her work to empower girls around the world. Debbie received her degree in engineering at Stanford University in 2005.

▮ JULIE WAINWRIGHT

Julie Wainwright is the founder and CEO of TheRealReal.com, the world's premier online luxury resale store. Julie is recognized as a strong CEO with deep experience in building consumer technology companies domestically and internationally. In 2013 she was voted one of the Most Admired CEOs in the San Francisco Bay Area by the *San Francisco Business Times*. Known for business creativity and her ability to focus the management team toward aggressive, high-performance goals, she has helped the companies she has run generate returns of over twenty times for investors.

Julie is a featured speaker at major industry conferences and universities, including Harvard University and Purdue University. Previous boards include Baker and Taylor, Wizards of the Coast, Berkeley Systems, Pets.com, Reel.com, The San Francisco Art Institute, Magic Theatre, and Headlands Center for the Arts.

▍ HEIDI ZAK

Heidi Zak is the cofounder of ThirdLove, an innovative bra and underwear brand based on the belief that fit should come first. In addition to offering signature half-cup sizes to provide a more precise fit, ThirdLove has developed a Fit Finder™ that empowers a woman to measure herself from home. Founded in 2013 and based in San Francisco, the company has raised over $13 million from investors, including NEA and Lori Greeley, the former CEO of Victoria's Secret. Prior to ThirdLove Zak cut her teeth in retail at Aeropostale, where she quickly rose to director of the retail giant, launching and running the International Division before moving over to marketing at Google. Zak holds an undergraduate degree in economics from Duke University and an MBA from MIT Sloan. In her free time she loves spending time with her two kids, breaking a sweat in boot camp class, and cooking with ingredients from San Francisco's farmers markets.

▍ MICHELLE ZATLYN

Michelle Zatlyn is cofounder and COO of Cloudflare, the web performance and security company. Today the company runs one of the world's largest networks, powering more than 10 trillion requests per month, nearly 10 percent of all Internet requests, for more than 2.5 billion people worldwide. Michelle holds a BS in chemistry and a minor in management from McGill University as well as an MBA from Harvard Business School.

▌ LUCY ZHANG

Lucy Zhang is a software engineer at Facebook. She is the cofounder of Beluga, a cross-platform mobile messenger that Facebook acquired in March 2011. Prior to Beluga Lucy helped design and develop products such as Google AdWords, Google News, and Google Docs.

Since leaving Google she has specialized in mobile app development. Lucy has a computer science degree from UC Berkeley.

NOTES

CHAPTER 4

1. Margarita Mayo, Maria Kakarika, Juan Carlos Pastor, and Stéphane Brutus, "Aligning or Inflating Your Leadership Self-Image? A Longitudinal Study of Responses to Peer Feedback in MBA Teams," *Academy of Management Learning and Education* 11 no. 4 (December 1, 2012): 631–652.

CHAPTER 5

1. Nancy M. Carter and Christine Silva, "Mentoring: Necessary but Insufficient for Advancement," Catalyst, 2010, www.catalyst.org/system /files/Mentoring_Necessary_But_Insufficient_for_Advancement_Final _120610.pdf.

2. Herminia Ibarra, Nancy M. Carter, and Christine Silva, "Why Men Still Get More Promotions than Women," *Harvard Business Review*, September 2010, https://hbr.org/2010/09/why-men-still-get-more -promotions-than-women.

CHAPTER 6

1. McKinsey & Company and Lean In, "Women in the Workplace 2016," September 2016, www.mckinsey.com/business-functions /organization/our-insights/women-in-the-workplace-2016.

2. Carlie Burlington, "Things My Male Tech Colleagues Have Actually Said to Me, Annotated," The Toast, April 1, 2015, http://the-toast.net /2015/04/01/things-male-tech-colleagues-have-actually-said-annotated.

3. "Item 10: I Have a Best Friend at Work," Gallup, May 26, 1999, www.gallup.com/businessjournal/511/item-10-best-friend-work.aspx.

4. Jay Smooth, "How to Tell Someone They Sound Racist," Ill Doctrine, July 21, 2008, www.illdoctrine.com/2008/07/how_to_tell _people_they_sound.html.

CHAPTER 7

1. "Breadwinner Moms," Pew Research Center, May 29, 2013, www .pewsocialtrends.org/2013/05/29/breadwinner-moms.

2. Meaghan O'Connell, "Don't Hide Your Maternity Leave," *New York Magazine*, October 27, 2016, http://nymag.com/thecut/2016/10 /death-sex-and-money-host-anna-sale-talks-maternity-leave.html.

3. Justin Wolfers, "A Family Friendly Policy That's Friendliest to Male Professors," *New York Times*, June 24, 2016.

CHAPTER 9

1. Sara Fisher Ellison and Wallace P. Mullin, "Diversity, Social Goods Provision, and Performance in the Firm," *Journal of Economic & Management Strategy* 23, no. 2 (Summer 2014): 465–481, http://economics.mit.edu/files/8851; Catalyst, "The Bottom Line: Connecting Corporate Performance and Gender Diversity," 2004, www.catalyst.org/system/files/The_Bottom_Line_Connecting_Corporate _Performance_and_Gender_Diversity.pdf; Pat Wechsler, "Women-Led Companies Perform Three Times Better Than the S&P 500," *Fortune*, March 3, 2015, http://fortune.com/2015/03/03/women-led-companies -perform-three-times-better-than-the-sp-500; Cindy Padnos, "High Performance Entrepreneurs: Women in High-Tech," February 1, 2010, www.w-t-w.org/en/wp-content/uploads/2013/09/High-Performance -Entrepreneurs-Final-4-9-UL.pdf.

INDEX

ABOUT THE AUTHOR

▮ **MAGDALENA YEŞIL** is a founder, entrepreneur, and venture capitalist of many of the world's top technology companies, including Salesforce, where she was the first investor and founding board member. Yesil is a former general partner at U.S. Venture Partners, where she oversaw investments in more than thirty early-stage companies and served on the boards of many. A technology pioneer, Yeşil founded three of the first companies dedicated to commercializing Internet access, e-commerce infrastructure, and electronic payments. UUnet, CyberCash, and MarketPay earned her the Entrepreneur of the Year title by the *Red Herring* magazine.

Yeşil is a founder of Broadway Angels, a group of female venture capitalists and angel investors. She is currently working on her fourth startup, DriveInformed, a technology company bringing trust and transparency to the auto finance industry. She serves on the board of directors of RPX, Smartsheet, and Zuora. Magdalena is an immigrant to the United States from Turkey and is of Armenian heritage. An avid hiker and sailor, she lives in San Francisco, California. (*Photo by Troy Wickett.*)

Visit her at www.magdalena.com
and follow @MagdalenaYesil on Twitter.